Reach Me with Smiles

A Handbook for Developing Disciple Makers

By Barbara A. F. Brehon

Reach Me With SMILES
Copyright © 2005 by Barbara A. F. Brehon
ISBN 1-891773-64-X

All rights reserved. No part of this publication may be reproduced, stored in a retrieval system, or transmitted in any form or by any means—electronic, mechanical, photocopy, recording, or any other means, now known or hereafter invented, without prior written permission from the author.

Scripture references taken from the New American Standard Bible © 1960, 1962, 1963, 1968, 1971, 1973, 1975, 1977, 1995, by the Lockman Foundation, Lahabra, CA. Used by permission.

All references to Greek origins and scriptural definitions taken from *The Hebrew-Greek Key Study Bible* (NASB), edited by Spiros Zodhiates, © 1990 by AMG Publishers.

Printed in the United States of America.

10   9   8   7   6   5   4   3   2   1

Publishing by Orman Press, Inc.
Lithonia, Georgia 30038

*Dedicated to the memory of my parents
Richard Thomas Fields, Sr.
and
Lillian Jerlean Watson Fields*

Contents

Foreword vii

Introduction ix
   Becoming A Teaching Church xii
   Building Visionary Leadership xiii
   Re-Visioning with Purpose xiii
   Recruiting and Cultivating Resources xv
   Choosing A Teaching Design and Curriculum xvi
   Moving Forward xvii

SMILES
   Stimulate 1
      Cultivating Deliberate Disciples 2
      Rediscovering the Joy of Teaching 3
      Creating an Atmosphere for Growth 4
      Asking Questions that Stimulate Discussion 6
      Facilitating through Small Groups 9
      Creating Images that Stimulate Growth 10
      Responding Responsibly 15
      Developing Teaching Techniques 17
      Applying Christian Teaching Techniques 20
      Differentiating Instruction 21

   Motivate 27
      Delivering Lessons that Motivate 27
      Choosing Appropriate Resources 32
      Motivating Teachers and Learners 33
      Training and Assessing Workers 38

Involve 43
    Teaching to Transform 43
    Teaching for Transfiguration 47
    Setting Goals and Objectives 52
    Improving Preparation Techniques 57

Love 63
    Demonstrating Love 64
    Applying Discipline in Love 65
    Dividing the Word Rightly 74
    Leading through Love 76

Encourage 79
    Teaching in Diversity 80
    Using Gifts for Disciple Making 83

Strengthen 89
    Moving Beyond Discipleship 90
    Making Disciples 91
    Strategizing for Disciple Making 93
    Increasing Teacher Effectiveness 94
    Studying the Word of God 97
    Reading the Word of God 99

Epilogue 103

References 107

Appendix A 111

Appendix B 115

Appendix C 119

Foreword

Clearly, one of the central functions of the church is teaching. I have read more books on Christian education than I can remember. Some have been very helpful and quite informative, while others have not been as informative. All claim to have a new twist on an old subject. The New Testament church took seriously the mandate of Jesus to disciple the world. In addition, this they did through their teaching ministries. Many churches give token consideration to the teaching function. One reason is the lack of resources that speak to the very heart of the task.

I have known Barbara Brehon for twenty-one years. I have watched God mature her into an outstanding Christian educator who has a deep passion and desire to do the will of God. Her book, *Reach Me With SMILES*, directly addresses the weekly task of teaching the Bible in the local church. Reverend Brehon has years of preparation and practice in the ministry of Christian education, especially in the teaching ministry of the local church. A teaching church will become a magnet for new converts, nurturing and developing them into committed disciples of the Lord Jesus Christ.

What is unique about this book? First, it is written by someone who is a practicing Christian teacher. Second, it is written for everyday Bible teachers who want a tool to improve their skills. Third, it addresses the how-to questions: How do I start a lesson? How do I stimulate a desire to learn more about God? How do I involve those I teach in the lesson? How do I love the people who sit with me week after week? How do I encourage my students? How do I strengthen them for the journey of faith? *Reach Me With SMILES* will challenge, encourage and instruct you in the fine spiritual art of sharing the Word of God with those who want to learn more about Jesus Christ.

As you read, allow the illuminating presence of the Holy Spirit to fill your mind and heart with new zeal for a great work!

> Geoffrey V. Guns, D.Min.
> Senior Pastor, Second Calvary Baptist Church
> Norfolk, Virginia

Introduction

Did you attend Bible classes as a child or teen? List in your mind the ways that you were taught as a child in Sunday School or a weekly Bible Study, public or private school. Compare and contrast those practices to methods used today. Be sure to consider available technologies, strategies and research about learning.

With these thoughts in mind, consider current practices in your church for teaching the Word of God. How is the Bible taught now? Is lecture the only format? How can a Bible lesson be taught to assist believers with spiritual growth? How can Christian educators reach students of the Word? They can reach them with SMILES! Teachers who use this concept will Stimulate, Motivate, Involve, Love, Encourage and Strengthen believers. Believers come to the learning environment saying, "Make me more curious about the Word of God." "Help me to study the Word of God." "Keep me coming to Bible classes regularly." "Discipline me, so that I am able to practice what I am learning by seeing it demonstrated in seasoned saints." "Lift me when I slip a little or fall." They also say, "Uphold me or be present with me when I am in need." Responding to each of these responsibilities will have an impact on the educa-

Reach Me With SMILES

tional ministry of a church. The chart below depicts the idea.

TEACHER	STUDENT	IMPACT
S timulate	*Make Me* become curious about the Word of God.	Interest
M otivate	*Help Me* study the Word of God.	Knowledge
I nvolve	*Keep Me* coming to Bible classes regularly.	Inclusion
L ove	*Discipline Me* so that I am able to practice what I am learning by seeing it in seasoned saints.	Model
E ncourage	*Lift Me* when I slip a little or fall	Reconciliation
S trengthen	*Uphold Me* and be present with me when I am in need.	Energy

The primary focus of *Reach Me With SMILES* is to answer one question: How can you teach a Bible lesson that will assist believers with spiritual growth? SMILES is an acronym that will help you improve your existing teaching skills. The SMILES concept recognizes that Christ is the center or focus of all teaching and the learners are second in priority. Teachers deliver the Word of God to their students so that they will grow or mature spiritually. To assist believers with spiritual growth, a Bible teacher should Stimulate, Motivate, Involve, Love, Encourage and Strengthen all believers.

The SMILES concept can be incorporated into teacher development or training sessions, focusing on one aspect at a time. The training may be weekly, monthly, or quarterly, depending on the needs of particular groups. However, monthly sessions are recommended to allow time for practice and self-evaluation before reviewing progress at general meetings.

An overview of the SMILES process and review of the specific aspect being emphasized may take place at regular teachers' meet-

Introduction

ings. The leader would facilitate discussions so that teacher strengths become building blocks and weaknesses are improved with the support of the team. Teachers should use *Reach Me With SMILES* with all learner groups, regardless of their age. When the teachers and learners blend or mesh, the impact is phenomenal (review the chart on the previous page).

As a teacher *stimulates* learning, students become interested and curious about the Word of God. When a teacher is motivated and *motivates* his students, knowledge and wisdom increase as the Word of God is studied. As a teacher teaches students how to study the Bible, believers will sense that the teacher is a learner, also. With intentional *involvement* of all persons in a weekly Sunday School or Bible Study class, attendance will become more consistent and steady. In a typical setting, class enrollment may be 12–20 persons and average attendance might be 5–9 students weekly. Attendance, at a glance, may not seem encouraging. However, when you take time to look at the frequency of an individual's attendance per month and dialogue with them about their personal study, you may find that learners are still in the Word weekly for personal devotions, growth and study.

Furthermore, one of the best techniques for reaching someone for spiritual growth is by modeling the desired outcome. The teacher leads by demonstrating a preferred behavior (such as Christian *love*) and the learners practice the biblical application in their everyday lives. The result will be Christians becoming reconciled to the Lord through the teacher's encouragement to continually walk in the way of the Word. When life becomes bumpy along the way, the teacher encourages the learners; the teacher lifts them by reminding them of the living hope that is found in Jesus (see 1 Peter 1:3).

The final stage in the development of the SMILES concept is to *strengthen* the learners, giving them the energy to press on in Christ. When we hold up the bloodstained banner of Christ we uphold the learners in whatever condition they present themselves.

Reach Me With SMILES

We are present with them when they are in need. As this process plays out, reciprocal relationships are built. The energy emitted from a group that has learned to demonstrate SMILES has Christ as its power source.

Using SMILES will help disciples become more effective disciple makers. Disciple makers are Christians who have consciously decided that they want to not only strengthen their personal relationship with Jesus, but also help others to grow. A disciple maker teaches others not only to follow, but also study the teachings of Jesus to become more like Him. This handbook is designed to help leaders goad persons who work with them along a path that is Christ-centered and other-centered. It will help disciples become more effective disciple makers, assisting non-believers or encouraging other believers to move toward Jesus. Effective disciple makers are able to teach people to develop a better relationship with Jesus. Sharing the Word of God with those who want to learn more is exciting and will keep you smiling.

Becoming a Teaching Church

The direction a church takes to become a teaching church should be based on the needs of that congregation within the community it serves. Teaching is the most important ministry of the church. Its goal is to improve the quality and effectiveness of Christian living and win others for Christ, as stated in Matthew 28:19–20. Church members should grow as a result of the teaching ministry. The maturity of Christians can be effectuated through a diverse teaching ministry under the leadership of a visionary pastor. In addition, whether a church is progressive and willing to make changes or not will effect its future. Therefore, Christian educators should continually assist the members of the congregation with envisioning new images that keep individuals focused on a biblical pattern for living. For example, following the Beatitudes, found in Matthew 5, will equip believers for daily living.

Introduction

Building Visionary Leadership

Visionary leadership and well-chosen resources can effectively move a church into a dynamic and relevant future. The *attitude* of the leadership in any church will affect the *altitude* of its teaching ministry. The term "leader" used here refers to the pastor in particular, or any person serving as head of a significant body within the local church. That could include the superintendent of the Sunday School or weekly Bible Study, the Minister or Director of Education, etc. The spiritual height of a church largely depends upon the degree of emphasis its leaders place on teaching the Word of God. When you consider the average weekly schedule in your church, how much time is allotted for teaching? In comparison, how much time is given to rehearsals (choir, ushers, etc.)?

A leader must keep the vision before the church. Where the church is going should be lifted higher than where the church has been. Though tradition is important to the vitality of a congregation, it must be tempered with the needs and direction of the membership. The congregation has to be taught that they can go beyond where they are to realize their potential. Therefore, leaders should be intentional about teaching them how to praise God. Praise nurtures hope and commitment to the Kingdom's work. It is not good to minister toward maintenance. Instead, keep a dream or a vision, out front to take the congregation beyond where they are.

Re-Visioning with Purpose

A church's teaching should center on building spirituality and faith in order to serve the people in the community. It should allow opportunities for learners to express their condition of existence and praise of God in view of their circumstances. Application of what is being taught should be the focus. A church will need to re-vision and train with intentionality. Teaching should be purposefully directed toward a specific desired outcome. It should be deliberately planned in ways to ensure that impressionable Christians are not easily persuaded by false doctrines, as stated in Ephesians 4:14.

Reach Me With SMILES

Moreover, pastors must realize that evangelism brings in new members with their own ideas regarding what the church should be. In order to keep the membership—seasoned and new members alike—working toward the same goals, teaching must be intentionally planned to reshape the old as well as mold the new.

The process of developing a church's new vision or tweaking an existing one should be shared between the pastor and the congregation to allow a sense of ownership by all. The greater the sense of ownership is evidenced in the majority or the core leaders of the congregation, the greater support and participation there will be. People are more likely to work toward a goal they help formulate. However, focus on the crucified Christ who ascended into heaven should never be compromised.

When a church leader re-visions, care should be taken to make the process meaningful for the people. It is important to use familiar language and updated worldviews. Diverse life experiences should be engaged so as not to limit the intelligibility of biblical, historical, and theological meanings for the average person. In other words, people are different. Engaging them requires diversity so that they experience multiple opportunities to learn. Individuals understand best through a variety of teaching styles. Leaders must provide opportunities and sources for meaning that answer the questions people are asking, since the people are on a quest for faith. Leaders or teachers should avoid using too many examples of their own life situations. While sharing personal testimonies or experiences with the Divine from your routine of the previous week is of critical importance, over emphasizing personal concerns can hinder the participation of others. People receive greater meaning when they participate in the process of teaching and learning. If a teacher realizes during the class session that his is the only voice being heard for an extended time, he should pose appropriate questions to encourage more student participation. Teaching should be student centered.

Using re-visioning to create meaning for people will result in a higher quality of living for God. This could mean establishing a full

Introduction

weekly schedule in lieu of Sunday-only programs. Pastors must promote teaching and learning in order for their congregations to cherish the value of Christian education. A church has to be taught how to be in relationship with God. In Joshua 4:6–7, the Israelites are told to inform their children of what the stones meant to them, thereby passing on, or teaching them how to be in relationship with God. Therefore, the ministry of the church should be organized around worship, teaching, and missions rather than separating them.

In Matthew 28:19–20, the goal of teaching is to make disciples. Intentional instruction should keep the vision of the church in view. Consequently, the members should receive training in what missions involves, how to do missions, how to evangelize, how to study the Bible, how to worship, and how to pray. Teaching that is concerned about a church's future should establish an on-going vehicle for growth in all of these areas, evidenced by higher levels of service encouraged by the church's leadership. In support of this idea, the writer of 2 Timothy 2:2 says that "the things individuals learn in the presence of many witnesses should be entrusted to those who are reliable and also qualified to teach others." Mediocrity is not acceptable when it comes to teaching God's people. Since teaching is a spiritual gift (Romans 12:6–8; 1 Corinthians 12:28–30), it simply is not acceptable to entrust teaching the Word of God to those who are not qualified.

Recruiting and Cultivating Resources

Besides visionary leadership, appropriate resources can effectively move a church into a dynamic and relevant future. One of the most valuable resources of any church is the people themselves, the teachers and the learners. It is an arduous task to keep co-laborers focused on God and rework a church's educational structure at the same time. The goal is improving the quality and effectiveness of Christian living to win others for Christ. When workers are enlisted, the goal must be kept in mind. Recruit and utilize teachers who not only possess the spiritual gift of teaching, but are also skilled in facilitating the discovery of a believer's connectedness to the biblical text. Christian educators must teach for meaning that is relevant to the learner rather than to the teacher.

Accordingly, teaching in any auxiliary in the church should invite learners of all ages to explore their own views as well as those found in Scripture. Teaching should prepare persons for life beyond of the walls of the church building, so that they can fulfill the Great Commission. Then, the learners will be able to take the lesson with them for application in their daily lives. Since people experience and define reality differently, the individual learner should be the focal point of the teaching as compared to the teacher.

Next, the relationship between people and their culture must be addressed. It is important that Christian educators be open-minded, flexible, and willing to change in order to reach learners for God. When I think about developing a teaching church, a vital consideration is a group of committed and dedicated workers who know God through the saving grace of Jesus Christ. Persons recruited to lead or teach must have experienced a connectedness of their own to the Bible. Moreover, Christian education goals and ministries cannot be maintained without adequately trained, experienced, and visionary core persons.

Choosing a Teaching Design and Curriculum

A particular design for the teaching church should be selected that enhances the goals of the church. A *developmental* teaching approach embraces a curriculum that encompasses various stages of development. Religious, moral, emotional, and cognitive development should be considered when choosing a curriculum that is sound. Christ-centered materials are a necessity for Christian teaching. These materials emphasize morals that are Bible-based. Concepts and activities in the curriculum should encourage students to probe introspectively with age-appropriate discussion questions. Tapping into emotions does not have to be any scarier than tapping into the mind for cognitive growth. Recognize the need for the

Introduction

materials to address the whole person and be ready to use the teacher to compensate for the areas not addressed. The teaching design should not only be developmental, but also life-centered. The Scriptures suggest a sequence to life and the teaching design employed by a church should intentionally optimize the motive behind all teaching in the church.

If the teaching or curriculum is not relevant to the students, the participation in the church's teaching opportunities will decrease and become stagnant. It is imperative to make a connection from ancient to contemporary times. One way to do this is by presenting the *kerygma* (life, death, and resurrection of Jesus) for personal identity, using tradition and Jesus stories. The aim of the teaching, then, is focused on spirituality rather than instruction for instruction's sake. Students must be helped to make life decisions based on the Christian story. Reflecting on positive and negative contemporary stories compared to Christian stories encourages the learners to make a link or connection from their current life situation to a parallel in the Bible. Teachers must facilitate those experience with creativity and flexibility, rather than relying on lecture alone. People need to be liberated from their present states of existence and the teaching process is more meaningful as well as more effective when it connects to the needs and interests of the learners.

Moving Forward

Several directions should have an impact on teaching for a dynamic and relevant future. Ministries should be based on meeting religious needs as the priority. People who move from church to church and new converts alike seem to be looking for the same thing. They appear to be on a quest for faith. A strong teaching ministry and commitment to discipleship will send people out to do ministry, providing opportunities for those on faith quests to experience lifestyles of faith.

To do this, the congregation must be able and willing to change in some respects in order to grow. This progressiveness should encompass a move from low expectation to high commitment communities of faith; low quality to high quality ministries; Sunday-program emphases to seven-days-a-week schedules. This progression should go from limited teaching to extensive teaching, from dull and boring worship to exciting experiences, which are not necessarily measured in decibels. Move from modest missions programs to missions organized around teaching and worship. Rather than organize around doing "good works," focus on feeding the spiritual needs of the membership. Progressive leadership and appropriate resources can effectively move a church into a future that is dynamic and relevant to the people.

Major problems of any direction chosen by the leadership to become a teaching church include volunteer and untrained teachers as well as inadequate curriculum. Before embracing a particular direction, a Christian educator should be careful not to ignore theology. Education with comprehensive goals does not compensate for a lack of theological value. Having information is one thing; the method of presentation toward the goal of the Great Commission is the other integral part of effective teaching.

In order to be considered a teaching church, there needs to be a commitment to growth. Since learning is a lasting change in a person brought about by experience, Christian educators must be concerned about spiritual growth. Those experiences provided by Christian education should be underscored with spiritual formation to help individuals grow and should not isolate individuals from the issues of the real world that they face daily.

Summary
- The direction a church takes to become a teaching church should be based on the needs of that congregation within the community it serves.
- The *attitude* of the leadership in any church will affect the *altitude* of its teaching ministry.
- Leaders must keep the vision before the church.

Introduction

- Teaching should center on building spirituality and faith in order to serve the people in the community.
- Applying what is being taught to daily life should be the focus.
- Pastors must realize that evangelism brings in new members who bring their own ideas with them regarding what the church should be.
- The process of developing a vision or re-visioning should be shared between the pastor and the congregation to allow a sense of ownership by all.
- Intentional instruction will keep the vision of the church in view.
- A church should select a teaching design that enhances the goals of the church.
- One of the most valuable resources of any church is the people themselves—teachers and learners.
- Teaching in any auxiliary of the church should invite learners of all ages to explore their own views as well as those found in Scripture.
- Both the teaching and the curriculum must be relevant to the learner.

Stimulate
Motivate
Involve
Love
Encourage
Strengthen

Stimulate

How do you teach a Bible lesson that will assist believers with spiritual growth? Believers come to us for instruction, saying, "Reach me by stimulating me." We must remember to always glorify God as we attempt to stimulate others. When we stimulate others we provide an atmosphere that evokes a desire to want more—a closer relationship with God, more time in studying the Bible, more intimate worship, more time in service to others in the name of Jesus.

People were created to be in relation with one another, not in isolation from one another. Why is solitary confinement within a prison considered a severe form of punishment? The importance of stimulation is at the root of the answer. This suggests that our teaching should not isolate. People who are depressed, deprived, depraved, disadvantaged, or at-risk have something in common—a lack of stimulation in their environment. When people come to church or a Bible study of any type, they expect or anticipate spiritual stimulation. They do not come so that they can leave in the same state of mind they were when they entered. The most effective Christian educators are those who are sensitive to creating learning environments that provide the proper stimuli for the specific needs that people bring. Would daily lectures with no other presentation style be acceptable to the parent of a public or private school student? Would you be satisfied with a child in this century being lectured to as the only means of receiving information for each year of their formal schooling? Adults are *children* of God, too. Following are some specific practices teachers can use to stimulate believers in God's Word.

Cultivating Deliberate Disciples
"Study to show thyself approved unto God, a workman that needeth not to be ashamed, rightly dividing the word of truth."
(2 Timothy 2:15)

As Christians, we are commanded to make disciples of all nations or to teach all nations. If our churches are going to be the churches that God intended, we must be intentional about preparing for this responsibility. Teaching is a spiritual gift of the Holy Spirit and we are obligated to nurture or develop it so that it can be used to the fullest potential in Jesus' name. Ultimately, everything we do must glorify the Father and edify the body of believers. Consequently, the role of the teacher is to make disciples of others. "Disciple-making" refers to what we do to assist others with spiritual growth while "discipleship" is personal. Are you growing? Are you in position to stimulate life-long learning and lasting spiritual growth in others?

Christian educators must want to attract and disciple non-Christians while we grow closer to the Father ourselves. Our discipleship causes us to witness to persons who have not yet accepted Christ as personal Savior. The same Christian, or disciple of Christ, must also want to be an effective disciple-maker of persons who have made a profession of faith in Christ. What does a disciple do to assist other disciples with their spiritual growth? Is this not deliberate or intentional teaching?

Stimulate

Deliberate disciples expect to increase in Christ-likeness, thus coming closer in relationship with God. As we seek to provide Christian nurture to others, we recognize a need to learn methods that are most effective for ministering to the souls entrusted to us. Therefore, the person who educates Christians helps others to grow in such a way that they are formed in the very image of Christ.

Rediscovering the Joys of Teaching

The joy of teaching comes when you see the light of understanding come over the faces of students or when you see changes in their talk. The joy comes when the quality of class discussions is eagerly and equally engaging week after week. Seeing enthusiasm in believers is matchless after you have spent hours preparing for them. Understanding that joy is a fruit of the Spirit, we must also acknowledge that the fruit of the Spirit must be developed in order for us to "live in the spirit" (Galatians 5:22–25). One way to develop your joy as a teacher is to prepare appropriate stimuli for the believers you teach. Failure to adequately prepare can cause dryness in your teaching. When the teacher becomes complacent and satisfied with the same methods and procedures, students tend to become bored, the energy and excitement of learning slowly dwindles and the joy is lost.

A practical education philosopher, John Dewey, said that if there is no learning there is no teaching. He was concerned with the whole person in a total situation. He did not believe that authoritarian methods offered contemporary people realistic preparation for life. He saw learning as problem solving. "He [the learner] must have an opportunity to select for himself, and then to attempt to put his own selections into execution that he may submit them to the only final test, that of action. Only thus can he learn to discriminate that which promises success from that which promises failure; only thus can he form the habit of relating his otherwise isolated areas to the conditions which determine their value." (Dewey, 1903)

The implication for a Christian educator is no different.

Reach Me With SMILES

Become a more effective teacher by developing a better understanding of the people you teach. Learn to manipulate the environment, not the Word of God, and rediscover the joy of teaching.

Insisting on one teaching style for all learners does not work very well. When we recognize the value of the experiences of others, we accept the importance of believers comfortably participating in a variety of learning activities without having to use extreme methods of coercion. I cannot make you what I want you to be, however, I can provide opportunities for the Word to show you what God is saying about your situation in life. I will not be aware of your situation if I use only one method or style of teaching that does not allow time to hear from you. The teacher as facilitator stimulates discussion groups. Discussion groups focus on the message or concept that the lesson lifts up for a given week. The point is to make sure that believers walk out knowing what Scripture has to say about a particular issue or concept. Change, or growth as a process, will have been facilitated with the Holy Spirit as the energizer.

Moreover, the Christian educator must emphasize more than processing information, even when the information is biblically based. Gestalt teaching suggests that learners perceive as a whole and respond to the elements that seem significant to them (*gestalt* is the German word for form or configuration). God allows access to information, technology and anything else under creation for His glory. Stimulation can sometimes occur simply by varying the structure of the learning environment. That could be physical, emotional or spiritual. Teachers, then, may have different responsibilities than previously perceived, not fewer. Consideration must be given to more than cognitive (thinking) processes.

Creating an Atmosphere for Growth

Would you continue to attend a class that was cramped or too hot all the time? Location and physical comfort play a vital role in creating an atmosphere that is conducive to spiritual growth. Would

Stimulate

you want to keep coming to a place to hear a message of hope in a packed-like-sardines room while the room next door is larger with lower attendance? Would you want to know more about Jesus when you are sitting in a cold place with your arthritis flaring up? When you think of a comfortable environment, several things are suggested: luxury, contentment, sufficiency, tranquility, rest, relaxation or nourishment. In addition to the biblical information that is presented, Christian educators address any or all of these factors at one time or another as we attempt to reach others for Christ.

What would be the best location for a class attended mostly by senior citizens or toddlers? Teens or middle-aged adults? When a group outgrows its space, reassign locations to insure a comfortable environment. While it is important to be organized, it is also important to understand the need for flexibility. Furthermore, it is good to have more than one plan that considers the needs of the people. People get used to "their" class meeting in a certain place. Before changing a location, show consideration for others by informing them of the impending move and the rationale behind the move. The mind needs time to relocate as well. By allowing for mental adjustment time, a better idea may spring forth.

According to educational research, both experience and perception play a role with the learning situation and learners' expectations of themselves. In churches, the people will not necessarily participate if their attitude toward the stimuli is negative. We do not have a captive audience, but rather a group of individuals who choose to be a part of the local gathering. We must learn techniques that stimulate people to want to know more about the Lord by placing value on who they are as created by God. Learning, then, is facilitated by the prior experiences of the learner. Learning is based on insight and a series of discoveries. In other words, learning by doing is key and effective teachers must structure the teaching-learning situation so that learning is stimulated. When believers are stimulated positively, the teacher's joy increases.

Meaningful conversations that emerge in class are well worth the effort expended to create the atmosphere for table talk. The depth for class discussion comes from the prior preparation of the teacher along with the presence of the Holy Spirit in the lives of the people present. The teacher uses the presence of the Holy Spirit, and their knowledge from preparation and experience, in addition to consideration of those who will be taught. Skillful teachers carefully crafts phrases to draw out of believers whatever the Holy Spirit needs. The combination creates a portable concept for the students.

Ask questions and present information to point to one key concept (not more than two) per week. It is simpler and easier to redirect students' "talk" toward the central idea of the week in this way. Keep in mind that it may take a little time to get a group used to the idea of not being lectured to week after week. I am not advocating the abandonment of the lecture method. However, it becomes less critical that the teacher makes each point prepared on the paper. The most important thing is that believers walk out with at least one spiritual concept to guide them and redirect their thoughts toward life-altering habits.

Discussions provide opportunity for clarifying personal beliefs. The classroom atmosphere enables the Holy Spirit to create confidence, which is needed to fight the battles of day-to-day living. The teacher can assist believers' spiritual growth by allowing opportunities for them to articulate their thoughts, knowledge and feelings. Learning that others have similar concerns and hearing how they handle situations stimulate believers' spiritual drive and fortifies their resolve to stay on the battlefield for the Lord. They can receive that from a gifted teacher, however, the application is stronger when multiplied by other persons in the class.

Asking Questions that Stimulate Discussion

Deductive approaches are less rigid and allow more flexibility; alternative hypotheses can be formulated. Hypotheses are general statements of explanation. They are tentative interpretations of complex ideas or biblical truths. Deductive questioning allows learn-

Stimulate

ers to discover the truth as they explore the logical consequences of a hypothesis. Develop a series of prepared questions from the concept or premise of the week. Let the questions lead the participants toward the suggested behavior or attitude that comes from the Bible lesson. The teacher is not the one to initiate the statements of truth. Leading questions are prepared that goad the believers along.

For example, let us say that the scriptural lesson is taken from Romans 10:14–17:

How then shall they call upon Him in whom they have not believed? And how shall they believe in Him whom they have not heard? And how shall they hear without a preacher? v. 15 And how shall they preach unless they are sent? Just as it is written, "How beautiful are the feet of those who bring glad tidings of good things!" v. 16 However, they did not all heed the glad tidings; for Isaiah says, "LORD, who has believed our report?" v. 17 So faith comes from hearing, and hearing by the word of Christ.

—NASB

Suppose the concept of the week is that faith grows by listening to God. A deductive method may begin with a scenario to illustrate the truth of the week followed by a series of questions. The teacher may choose to ask questions similar to the following, prior to reading the Scripture, to stimulate the lesson.

Deductive Questions for Participants

1. What is faith?
2. From where does faith come?
3. Give an example of how growing faith is demonstrated. Be sure to use words that describe specific observable actions.
4. When is the last time God spoke to you? What did He say? Where were you when it occurred? Spend this week reading at least one verse from the Bible. Then, sit still for a moment. Write down your thoughts after you have been

quiet for a while, thinking about the verse. Your thoughts during this time may tell you what God is saying to you.

Imagine the excitement that can be generated when believers uncover biblical truths as compared to being told those truth with little time provided for them to wrestle with it.

On the other hand, inductive questioning provides the hypothesis or the biblical truth. A generalization is a concluding statement that represents a tentative solution to a problem based on available information at the time. The teacher may use this approach to pinpoint a specific truth that is the focus of the scriptural lesson. Activities and discussions are developed that draw this hypothesis or biblical truth out of the believers.

For example, the concept of the week from Romans 10 is clearly stated initially by the teacher: Faith grows by listening to God. The Scripture would probably be read early in the lesson. The teacher may pose questions such as these:

Inductive Questions for Participants
1. Tell us about a time when you listened to God.
2. Share with the class an experience where you did not consult God first.
3. What are some things you can do to improve your ability to hear God?
4. What verses in the lesson today will help your faith to grow more this week?

No rule says that you have to approach each lesson the same way. Let the theme of the passage or the concept of the day determine the specifics as the Holy Spirit directs you. Discussions that lead to self-reflection tend to cause believers to spend more time outside of class sessions reading and re-reading the lessons. They like the way it makes them feel from the inside out and want to have something to contribute when given another opportunity.

Stimulate

When leading discussions, inquiry teachers consider questions that stimulate or energize the conversation. Feel free to ask spontaneous questions that stem directly from current conversations on the floor. However, only ask questions to which you really want to know the answer. You will be able to show that you care about the learners. There should by no "devil's advocate" questions in this teaching strategy. Instead, the teacher could use question stems such as these:

What led you to say that?
What evidence in the Scripture supports that idea?
Show me where you see that?
Do you agree that…?
Do you agree with his point that…?
Student 1, tell Student 2 why you disagree with her opinion.
What do you mean by that?
Why do you think she did that?
How is that? When is that the case? Why is that?

Facilitating through Small Groups

Most teachers regularly run out of time to cover the points that they want to emphasize each week in class. Facilitating small groups within the class is one way of increasing time for discussion. Asking poignant questions and giving students an opportunity to wrestle with those questions stimulates spiritual growth as they seek biblically-based answers. Choosing the best question for a specific lesson requires that you consider the meaning of the passage of Scripture being studied and the contemporary issue to be addressed or resolved. Plan at least four questions to centralize the discussion on the topic of the week. Moreover, it is natural that other questions will emerge as the lesson is presented and believers interact.

Small groups are usually safe places for everyone to share experiences or concerns. Believers who need more spiritual support gain it by participating in small groups. The teacher as facilitator not only keeps the discussion groups stimulated, but also redirects believers when they stray too far from the concept being emphasized. For example, you could say, "I didn't think of it that way. Tell us how that is connected to growing faith" (or whatever is the theme of the week).

Bonding, caring, trusting and inquiring are products of the time spent developing this approach to teaching the Bible. It takes time to cultivate it. Just like God gives us time after time to get our relationship right with Him, we need to invest the necessary time to stimulate our students. As the needs of believers are met, life-altering decisions can be made. After all, what we want is a lifestyle change that leads others to Christ. When believers see the Word lived out in the lives of the teacher and other people in the class, a lively hope exists that makes it attainable for them, too.

Creating Images that Stimulate Growth

I challenge Christian educators created in the image of God to use knowledge for God's glory when teaching God's Word. Many believers would comprehend more if they were taught to use images based on their experiences. The idea of using illustrations is certainly not new. When our teaching gets stale, though, images can be refreshing. Images that occur to the teacher while privately reading sentences in the Bible should be used to illumine the lesson to be covered. These images or mental pictures are portable. A picture is worth more than a thousand words.

How do you create images that stimulate? Show believers how they can take the pictures created in their minds with them for life application. Talk about how an image came to you and how it made an impact at a specific time for you. One caution: As you share about yourself, keep it brief. The apostle Paul is an example of one who made a point using a personal experience, but kept the details to himself. We still do not know what his "thorn in the flesh" was. However, we do know the biblical truth that Christians must not be conceited or self-exalted (2 Corinthians 12:7). Let us look into a

Stimulate

rationale that further supports this approach.

B. F. Skinner, well known for behavior modification techniques, suggests that behavior is influenced by what learners say to themselves in inner speech. One can change the behavior of others by helping them change this inner dialogue. The implication for Bible teachers would be to provide biblical models for learners to imitate, for example, pointing out the rewards for a character read about in a particular passage. Paul is one biblical example, just mentioned, that illustrates a model teachers can use for sharing personal testimony. To employ the implication from Skinner, the teacher would provide reinforcement when a desired change is evident. You can know the change in the believer has occurred from their personal testimonies, not your own supposition or judgment. Offer support to reinforce the changed behavior and give demonstrative praise to God in class for the evidence of that change.

There are other implications for Christian educators who know that God created us in His image. We know that each of us possesses innate abilities that are uniquely crafted each time God chooses to form someone in the womb. According to educational research, the right side of the brain controls a portion of our personality. Right-brain thinkers are more creative and not necessarily verbal. This research is not new. This 1970s model of brain systems has been updated to include eight brain systems:

Linguistic	-	use of language
Logical	-	use of reason
Spatial	-	use of the body (the person) in relation to other things around it to get the big picture
Kinesthetic	-	use of the sense of touching
Musical	-	use of creativity of expression
Interpersonal	-	use of relationships between two people
Intrapersonal	-	use of relationships with a broader range of persons outside of the group
Naturalist	-	use of the environment

Reach Me With SMILES

How can the average teacher of the Bible use any of these or any combination of these models to develop a theme or a biblical truth?

1) Consider the idea that poor readers are better at relational thinking than analytical thinking.
2) Consider the possibility of asking *"What if...?"* after teaching or *"How did it make you feel?"*
3) Imagine the creativity of people who are nonverbal or quiet.
4) Show the geography of a passage in a concrete, non-rational manner from time to time.
    a) Simply use a map. Have a large one available rather than asking students to use the one in their Bibles. (Students may not have maps in the Bibles they brought with them.)
    b) If someone has traveled to similar places, let them share.
    c) Show pictures using the computer and LCD projector. There is so much available software.
5) Clustering or grouping details helps learners visualize the big picture.
    a) Spatial ideas require intuitive or divergent thought and are holistic.
    b) Find the emotions or the gutsy experiences in the lesson and explore with prepared questions whether these are accepting, visionary or only a dream.

The right brain can also synthesize left-brain information in a gestalt (very structured) versus holistic manner. Remember that Gestalt teaching suggests that learners perceive as a whole and respond when it is significant to them. When we present whole forms, we use gestalt strategy. In other words, part of your brain can figure out information the other part receives. The gifted teacher recognizes that there are differences in the proportions of

Stimulate

either mode the students they teach use to process or to learn. The gifted teacher does not try to figure out who learns which way best. The Holy Spirit handles that. The teacher simply varies the presentation style so that various modalities are used. The likelihood is that more people will be reached with diverse stimuli.

Left-brain thinkers are verbal and more relational. They are more analytical and have rational, logical thought. This may create linear thinkers who may need outlines. People with these tendencies are convergent and logical thinkers who theorize and appear to be critical or all-knowing. It is important that the Christian educator stimulate the thinking of *all* believers for Christ. Some believers you can predict to be realistic, authoritative, scientific or conformist. Do not let this pose a problem for you. Patterns of reasoning can develop from the Scriptures as you let the Holy Spirit tell you what questions to ask; the Holy Spirit can reach every type of thinker in the room. There are times to be a relational facilitator; then there are times when logical sequences need to be integrated. Ask the Holy Spirit to guide you through that.

Know that learning is individualized. You cannot learn for me any more than I can learn for you. Nevertheless, *if* I could teach you, couldn't you learn? Then teach as if you know this as truth.

Points to Ponder

- Pray that the Lord will show you how to stimulate *all* of His people that you teach for His service. He knew them when He formed them.
- Examine yourself and pray for God's guidance for lesson planning.
- Use measurable and universal language for the people you teach.

—continued

- Choose words that are easily understood by all and draw responses that allow the participants to see the Lord at work in their own lives.
- Teach to each one.
- *WARNING: Individualized teaching may increase your preparation time!*

Practice

- Read Psalm 139:1–18, 23–24.
- As you communicate with God through Jesus Christ:
    - Examine yourself.
    - Consider themes or concepts, then choose one or two.
    - Think about modalities that help people learn.
    - Plan a lesson that uses multiple modalities.

Sample Inquiry Method Questions Based on Acts 1:1–14

v. 4–5	Do you recall an experience of leaving a place and wishing you had stayed a little while longer? Share it.
v. 6–7	What might happen if you got something back that had been taken away from you? (house, jewelry, job, spouse, etc.)
v. 7	What would it really be like to know everything?
v. 8	What two things must you know?
v. 9–11	How do you stop fixing your attention on inappropriate things? What is your sky?
v. 12–13	Where do you have to go to go back to your Jerusalem (going back to wait on the Holy Spirit, mentally or physically)?

Stimulate

Responding Responsibly

In order to keep believers stimulated, be aware of the responses you give as well as the questions you ask. Value statements can harm the hard work you put into planning a session. The trick of the enemy is to have you unaware of judgmental things you might say. For example, a student has just finished speaking and you say, "That's good." Somebody else had previously articulated something and you did not really say anything; you just went to the next part of the lesson. This person may wonder if you thought something was wrong with what they shared. Hers was "good," so mine must have been "bad." It is certainly not your intention to judge anybody. However, a weaker mind may perceive it that way as Satan tries to enter. Remember, even the strongest Christian has weak moments. Using language that judges students' answers or statements as valid or invalid may quench the Spirit of God.

- Avoid thinking in terms of right versus wrong.
- Focus the conversation on the text being read.
- Remember to be a teacher who facilitates and inquires.
- Remember to allow conversation that does not center around the teacher.
- Prepare questions in advance.
- Avoid answering the questions you ask.
- Erase the impression that the right answers must come from the teacher.

Learners may not value what the teacher is talking about. Teacher responses can be questions. How can you phrase an appropriate question that redirects the thinking and refers believers back to the Bible? We can reach believers in three domains or areas:

1. Affective (emotional)   -   *How does it make you feel?*
2. Cognitive (intellectual)   -   *What does it make you think of?*
3. Psychomotor (behavioral)   -   *What can you do to show...?*

Reach Me With SMILES

Recognize that God reaches people spiritually. Teaching is often cognitive (mental without spiritual emphasis); no wonder people dropout and stop coming. To counteract this, conduct quarterly self-evaluations and class valuations. *Evaluation* is an individual's judgment of himself—students and teachers alike. A *valuation* refers to something of value, what it is worth. Is your teaching valuable? Is there evidence of the movement of the Holy Spirit in the lessons and your students' lives? Paul wrote in 2 Corinthians 13:5, "examine yourself." Evaluate yourself. Give students the opportunity to express their opinion about their growth, study and progress as well as the process used to teach the class. How do we know if there is learning if we do not build in assessment strategies? What we do to determine our own effectiveness as teachers should not prohibit growth. What we do must enhance the growth of individuals for Christ. WARNING: *Do not ask the question if you are not ready to hear the answer and do something about it!*

Understand that each person in any class is operating at a different level. Spiritual, cognitive (intellectual), affective (emotional), psychomotor (behavioral), social, economic, and self-esteem are all levels that vary. The variations are not only from person to person but also within any one person. No one has a high, medium, or low level of all. Your format or content at a given time may be inappropriate or not on the proper level for someone. That one sheep or the group needs diversity to attain and retain your point. Use techniques to reach everyone with different levels of questioning. How do you determine the appropriate level for any of the areas mentioned? Keep it simple. Ask the questions that you want answered.

Many things point to being an inquiry teacher. Avoid asking questions for the sake of asking. Avoid giving the impression that you do not want or care about students' answers. Do not produce inappropriate information or judgments about the people you teach. Think of it like this: Teaching in the church does not provide captive audiences. When the natives get restless or offended they flee. Consequently, the teacher may be left with fewer and fewer people

Stimulate

in attendance. Devil's advocate questions have no place here.

Turn the learners into discoverers; make them ask you to tell God's story (Joshua 4:19–24). Show the geography of God's glory. He can move today in our lives—His territory—in the same way He did in ancient times, if we trust His leadership and obey His commandments. If God says do not do something, then don't. If God says do it, then do it. If God says not at all, forget it! (Joshua 11). Let the Lord have His way.

How can you teach a Bible lesson that will assist believers with spiritual growth? Teachers should Stimulate, Motivate, Involve, Love, Encourage and Strengthen all believers. Stimulate learning so that learners become interested and curious about the Word of God. When a student is stimulated there is an apparent attitude that says, "Make me want to know more about the Word of God." The impact for the teacher who receives this attitude would be the interest of the student in continuing to be a part of that teaching-learning situation. The teacher should stimulate all learners regardless of the age of the group. When the teacher and learners mesh the impact is phenomenal.

Developing Teaching Techniques

The most effective Christian educators merge how to study the Bible with how to apply it in daily life. Effective teaching techniques emerge as the Holy Spirit births to freshness in your planning. While you are teaching, intentionally use the words that show what you do when you read and study the Bible. Use the words *observe*, *interpret*, or *apply*, then break down their meanings:

> Observe: *What does the verse actually say?* You might ask students to identify words that name people or ideas, words that show action, or words that express emotion. What did the person do or what does the verse say that God did? The point is to get into the wording of the text.

Reach Me With SMILES

Interpret: *What did that verse mean when it was written?* Consider the person who wrote it. Then consider what it meant to the people who heard it or read it. Explore the context of the verse or passage. One way to pull out particularities of the context is with the acronym PERCS, which stands for the Political, Economic, Religious, Cultural, and Social dynamics prevalent at the time of the writing. When a Bible student considers a combination of these factors in the text, deeper understanding of biblical truths results.

Apply: *What does the text mean today?* Now is the time to transport what it said and what was happening then to contemporary thoughts. Bring the life of the reader to the discussion. We discuss at length in the pages to come how to apply scriptural truths to the lives of your students. Application is the core of *Reach Me With SMILES*. Christian educators who model the concepts they teach are most effective.

- Let learners know that you care enough to let the Holy Spirit uncover how they learn best. Stimulate each other and rediscover the joy of teaching.
- Present information and concepts in ways that challenge learners to think for themselves.
- Show students how to read the Word of God and communicate with God while in private personal study at home.
- Make learners ask for more.

Martin Buber, another icon who influenced educational philosophy, developed the thought that *dialogue* confirms both participants as having unique value. These mutual relations give students confidence to think for themselves. By engaging students in dialogue, a teacher or facilitator can lead believers to choose between alternatives. The Christian educator should likewise assist believers in becoming active conversationalists with classmates and God, never

Stimulate

closing their minds or hearts, seeking more profound truths than they already possess

Stimulate the conscious by using all the senses. Tactile experiences are those things that require the sense of touch. There are times when a lesson comes more alive because the teacher gives an opportunity for believers to actually touch one another to express care and compassion. Another way to use touching in a lesson would be to have objects that represent ideas. For example, feeling the fuzz on a peach during a discussion on the fruit of the spirit would be a reminder that others see what is produced when you grow in the Lord. Persons who are not verbal learners remember object lessons longer.

Kinesthetic teaching provides the use of other senses jointly. How many of the five senses can you use to demonstrate or illustrate one concept or biblical theme? A combination of hearing, touching, seeing, smelling and tasting can be used in many lessons to avoid the strict lecture delivery method. Shift gears in teaching; give students something different in tone (activity). Hook up teaching to muscles and music. Make students move to point out a topic. Illustrate a topic through song. Teach problem solving skills rather than providing the answer to every question you raise. Ask students to demonstrate what they would do if they were a character in the lesson. Give them an opportunity to plan, then role-play it. Allow discussion that lets the observers share feelings and images that were invoked while listening.

Know that imagery is creative imagination and allows people to visualize while they read, or paint a mental picture after reading. Teach in a way that gives learners opportunities to describe their imagery. This gives them the chance to share how they feel about situations in life and make appropriate responses when faced with similar situations in the future.

Invite believers to compose and envision their own knowledge. Give believers opportunities to clarify their thinking and challenge one another's thinking. Allow them to teach each other while "the teacher" acts as facilitator of the process.

You could dare to have adults actually draw or paint a picture—yes, even adults—in order to stimulate discussion. Put into pictures what cannot be put into words. Rejuvenate them with word association, clustering or webbing to generate relationships. Many of the believers we teach could effectively assist us, since some of them have used a plethora of techniques at their workplace or in school.

It is obvious that the ideas presented here will not work well without some degree of student preparation. They need to read and study prior to coming to class as well. They need to actively take notes or journal the thoughts the Holy Spirit gives them outside of the class setting. They might just do that if they know that they will have opportunities to share and ask questions in class sessions. The most inquisitive believers become your helpers and care should be given when organizing small groups to avoid putting the inquirers in the same group. Try becoming an inquiry teacher and rediscover the joy of teaching.

Applying Christian Teaching Techniques

The effective teacher is a steward of God's time. Time management and lesson planning include prepared questions, activities, projects, etc. A well-planned lesson includes a variety of approaches to learning coupled with enthusiasm. Get fired up about studying. Grow in grace with planning. Recognize that your personal study time and lesson planning time are separate entities. Let the Holy Spirit control the climate of your classroom and stay fired up about teaching with diversity. The sky is the only limit!

Use a theological approach with a variety of techniques. *Theology* is the belief system or faith stance that guides your convictions. It is the study of God and godly things. As a Bible teacher, you must be aware of your personal position with the Word and how the Holy Spirit is able to manifest itself through that Word to reach people for God. Thus, a theological approach is one that begins

Stimulate

with faith that Jesus will guide you to the specific delivery style that is needed to reach the people who will be present that day in a particular context. That process begins with the teacher; the preparer's heart must be pricked and pierced by the Spirit of God.

Some churches use a specific curriculum that provides the lesson aim and have a staff person, the pastor or designee, who reviews the lessons in teachers' meetings. This does not excuse the teacher from personal prayer, moments of meditation and time-consuming table work required for executing God's plan. Spend time considering the background and general characteristics of your students.

How can you teach a Bible lesson that will assist believers with spiritual growth? Incorporate them and their needs in planning and delivering the lesson. Students know how they learn best; hear them.

Differentiating Instruction

Are there students in your class who repeat everything you or their classmates say? Though it may be irritating at times, realize its probable purpose. Perhaps they are *verbal* learners who need to mouth ideas themselves to be certain they have grasped them. Prepare specific activities to capture the verbal student in a way that does not hinder the class. If you know that oral or outspoken persons will be present, plan for them in a manner that meets their need. Be aware of verbal learners as literal thinkers. Avoid using rhetoric. Using clichés, jargon, popular phrases or examples that simply seem to fit does not add to the exposition of the Bible. If it comes out in the course of your presentation, that's one thing; just be aware of how you are using language. Rhetorical statements or examples that you use may be taken textually or exactly as you say them. Because believers come to class at different stages of spiritual maturity, it is difficult to determine when a common expression you use may be taken literally because of your role as a Bible teacher. This further supports that variety in your teaching style or technique is necessary. More people are reached in their context when a variety of approaches are utilized.

Some believers are not really quiet by nature, but in class they will not speak up. They sit quietly rather than participate actively. They may be learners whose dominant learning modality is hearing or *auditory*. They listen and thereby seize the acoustics of the context. They need to sit back and absorb all that goes on like a sponge. From time to time, they will speak out for clarification, having apprehended in part. When a teacher is *person-minded* while planning lessons, the need to blend auditory, verbal and visual methods of presentation is apparent.

Some people are good with their hands. As they explain what they are trying to say, they use their hands to shape it. They can make things and do things with their hands that amaze us. They probably learn best that way, too. *Kinesthetic* learners need to make contact with a concept. If they can literally handle it, they will understand it or grasp it more quickly. How can we get students to touch something that represents the main idea of the lesson? What can they hold? The Holy Spirit will answer as you meditate.

Realize that using illustrations goes beyond pictures with words. Visual representations or icons help people perceive the truths of God sometimes more clearly than words. What images come to mind while you are studying and how can you use available resources to depict them? Who in your class needs to see something in order to make a personal connection? How can you show them what the Scripture of the week says? The Spirit of God will answer as you take time to meditate.

Many things have analogous relationship; that is, two things can be compared that are not normally associated with one another. Such comparisons appeal to *visual* learners because they are ocular people who need to be able to see things for themselves. Ocular refers to people who benefit most from illustrations, diagrams, charts and the like. The teacher must provide experiences where concepts can be observed. The teacher uses phrases from the text to show similarities or likenesses and differences. Comparisons are

Stimulate

used as symbols that allude to our Christ-likeness. We have been created differently, but in the image of one God; we try to imitate His Son so that we can some day be with the Father. It is fitting to use imagery and symbols or objects to represent the concepts in the biblical lessons that we teach. When preparing a lesson, take the time to pray for the Holy Spirit to show you which image to demonstrate. Remain focused on one, not more than two, concepts for one week.

Imagine one lesson, the concept of the week, one verbal technique, one auditory method, one kinesthetic form and one visual image. When presented in one block of time, more persons present will be reached for Jesus. Of course, all of these may not apply to the lesson at hand each week. Nevertheless, I urge you to always utilize differentiated instructional techniques. People learn best in a variety of ways. The point is that our teaching style should reflect an understanding that God created us differently and we are required to teach His Word to all of His people.

Practice

Use the following verse to identify a teaching technique you can use in a lesson plan for your students. Apply as many of the following modes as possible to guide your thinking. They are presented in random order.

Let your light so shine before men, that they may see your good works, and glorify your Father which is in heaven. Matthew 5:16.

Dialogue _____

Tactile _____

—*continued*

Reach Me With SMILES

Kinesthetic _____

Theological _____

Verbal _____

Auditory _____

Person-minded _____

Visual _____

Summary

The most effective Christian educators merge how to study the Bible with how to apply it in our lives. If we can do that, effective teaching techniques will emerge as the Holy Spirit gives birth to freshness. You teach people; you teach people the Bible with Jesus as the center of the lessons. Ask yourself, what is it about this young lady or this gentleman, boy or girl that I need to reach today for Christ? Did I feed him or her last week? Will I feed them with the lesson that I am preparing now? How do I make it portable for them?

- Develop an atmosphere that is conducive to believers such that they feel free to be expressive without being judged.
- Be intentional about having time to build relationships with each lesson.
- Let the lessons draw students out rather than drag them along.
- Use materials to accentuate or give emphasis to the lesson.
- Meditate daily, paying attention to any images revealed by the Holy Spirit.

Stimulate

- Practice reading the Bible for yourself before reading it to prepare for teaching.
- Become an inquiry teacher who uses inductive and deductive reasoning.
- Know that learning is individualized.
- Become a more effective teacher by developing a better understanding of the people you teach.
- Learn to manipulate the environment, not the Word of God, and rediscover the joy of teaching.
- Remember that when believers are stimulated positively, the teacher's joy increases.
- Prepare questions and presentations to point to one, and not more than two, concepts per lesson.
- Understand that it may take a little time to get a group used to the idea of not being lectured to week after week.
- Structure lessons so that believers will walk out with at least one spiritual concept to guide and redirect their thoughts toward life-altering habits.
- Keep believers stimulated. Be aware of the responses you give as well as the questions you ask.

Practice

Reconsider a basic Bible study method: observe-interpret-apply. Use it as an outline for various stimulating techniques to deliver a lesson. Before you plan the lesson for others, make it personal.

—*continued*

Practice

Identify God's plan in each passage below. Choose one to develop into a lesson. Concept: Jesus had a plan. Do we?

Acts 1: 4–8
Galatians 4:1–7
Ephesians 1:3–20

Further Reading

Anderson, Lorin W., ed. *International Encyclopedia of Teaching and Teacher Education.* Pergamon, 1995.

Armstrong, Thomas. *Multiple Intelligences in the Classroom.* Association for Supervision and Curriculum Development, 2000.

Orlich, Donald C., et al. *Teaching Strategies: A Guide to Better Instruction.* D. C. Heath, 1980.

Yount, William R. *Called to Teach: An Introduction to the Ministry of Teaching.* Nashville: Broadman and Holman Publishers, 1999.

Motivate

How do you teach a Bible lesson that will assist believers with spiritual growth? Believers who come to us for instruction are saying, "Reach me by motivating me." When a teacher is motivated and motivates learners, knowledge and wisdom increase because the Word of God is studied. Instructors show learners how to study the Bible and believers can sense that the teacher is a learner, also.

Delivering Lessons that Motivate

Teaching for learning is a process. An effective teacher knows what he or she is teaching and why it is being taught. Goals are set to specifically enhance the Scripture at hand. Christian teachers teach to enrich lives for Christ and emphasize results based on a Christian theological approach. A Christian teacher knows how to draw the most out of believers through a variety of techniques as they reach the ultimate goal of reconciliation and relationship with God. Varied teaching techniques give believers multiple opportunities to use the lesson to help someone else. Therefore, time management and lesson planning are very important to guiding a person toward spiritual growth.

Reach Me With SMILES

It takes time to identify age-appropriate activities that focus on the one message a lesson will bring out to a particular group of believers. The art of asking questions is critical to a good lesson with meaningful discussion. Projects for all ages can be discerned so that the learners can make it personal and take it home. Using intergenerational and cooperative lessons, from time to time, helps believers to become connected to one another as they learn to connect with Christ. If these activities and projects are service oriented, imagine the bigger benefit of ultimately reaching others for Christ!

Now, let us assume that your church is a teaching church. This means that teacher effectiveness is increasing and the teachers are personally prepared to teach each lesson. One part of lesson preparation that may often be overlooked is for teachers to visualize or imagine following through with a lesson before actually teaching it.

Imagine the following:
- You arrive early enough to set up the classroom for the lesson.
- You arrange the chairs to accommodate the day's activities, since they will vary from week to week.
- You write the lesson outline on the board, place the first transparency on the overhead projector, prepare the LCD projector and computer, display the appropriate maps, etc.
- You set up any material, prop, or resource you will use before students arrive, so that you are mentally available to be person-minded with believers as they enter.
- As students arrive, start them sharing about their past week as general conversation. Only two people may be present at the time, but start by talking about the week. There may be a testimony, praise, or personal struggle; things may come up that need to be handled spiritually. Intentionally allow this time at the beginning of class weekly so that needs and concerns do not have to travel around with the students or the teacher for another week.
- Take the opportunity to make a connection to the previous

Motivate

week's message conversationally and go into the lesson of that day. Also, always start class on time. The conversation is part of the class. Students may want to get there so they do not miss anything.

- Create an atmosphere where students feel comfortable bringing any reaction to your attention that may be leftover from the previous week and their needs can be addressed.
- You may use Prayer as the official beginning of the lesson, however, it does not have to be the first thing on your lesson plan.

As this procedure becomes routine, some believers will look forward to the time of sharing and become more punctual. As the teacher becomes more person-minded, a sincere concern to know who these people really are and what they like to do emerges. Who likes to go fishing? Maybe some can get together and go fishing sometime. You cannot fish in your classroom, but look at the relationships that can be built while on a pier or the shore. Have a fellowship outing to the movies. Alternatively, you may have the class over to your house for a fellowship meal or dessert. Choose a person who may be naturally suited as a fellowship leader to be responsible for organizing a quarterly outing. People will feel included and develop a commitment to the class. Christian bonding and nurturing will develop.

If you are really teaching, you are trying to effectuate or facilitate a change in the believers. Consequently, teaching in the church should invite learners to explore their own views and those found in Scripture. That does not have to happen in the church house. Enabling learners to take the lesson with them and apply it to their daily lives results from having time to explore their thoughts as they reflect on scriptural lessons. The relationship between a person and his or her culture can be addressed and those who have been on a faith quest, needing new friends for a new lifestyle, will begin to feel victory in Jesus. An open-minded and flexible facilitator is willing to change in order to reach learners for God.

Reach Me With SMILES

Think about how you teach the Bible. Didn't Jesus socialize? He was often at a celebration; He worked hard on the Father's behalf and went on retreats. Do you remember that He stopped by Mary, Martha and Lazarus' house? If Jesus took time like that, why shouldn't we fellowship with other believers? We are not like Jesus, but we are trying to be like Him. We have different gifts, abilities and interests; we are individuals who like to go to different places. Until we become like Jesus we will work on His behalf with what has been given to us. In the meantime, we will work toward the ultimate goal. When we get to be like Him we will go to be with Him face to face.

Once the informal discussions at the start of the class have taken place, the facilitator should make an appropriate transition to move into the lesson, starting with prayer time. Whether all the information prepared is covered is less important than the people feeling fulfilled and complete when they leave on fire for the Lord. When this happens, the teacher has done the job for the week, even though the plan may not have been covered in its entirety. The lesson was delivered, not only with a connection to the previous week, but also with relevance toward the one message that came out of the Scripture of the week. The Holy Spirit took charge.

Do not force feed or overload the students. Give believers the amount of information, mixed with application, that they can carry out of the door with them. Teaching Sunday School or a weekly Bible Study isn't like grocery shopping. When you shop for groceries, you can buy many bags of things and carry a trunkload home with you. When you get to your residence you can go back to the car as many times as necessary until you take all the groceries inside. Give people an opportunity to reflect and receive within their soul what they can bear. Now, they can use it when they walk out. Focus on one topic or theme per lesson and develop it, using as many different activities and discussion enhancers as possible in the time frame. Do not frustrate the soul with too much at one time. They may stop coming, continue a faith quest elsewhere, or choose

Motivate

to be fed by someone else because they experienced no victory.

Reinforce one point at a time. Pause intentionally, taking twenty to thirty seconds of silence so that the Holy Spirit can let the Word sink in. Let a thought sit with people instead of rushing to the next point because you have a schedule to keep. The most important thing is that believers get what they need for that week. The next week, don't try to play catch up with what you didn't cover. It is not your show. You can assume that believers are keeping up with the reading and studying at home. You affirm their participation. As you go on with the next lesson, remember that you can use conversation during the time at the beginning of the next session to tie up loose ends. Maybe some re-teaching needs to take place.

Another approach is to start by presenting information and lead to the lesson aim. Provide time for shared experiences and very brief testimonies of the past week, then ask a simple question. It could be the lead to the lesson. For example, suppose the discussion from the previous lesson asked the relevant question, "What are you really all about?" The next lesson could begin, "As we talk about our lesson today, I really want you to consider what you are all about." Remember, that was the question that framed last week's lesson and in a sequential study (a series of lessons from a specified curriculum), the teacher may add variety from ending with a question by beginning with one. Students receive the connectedness and are more readily prepared to be engaged from week to week.

Yet another way to initiate the session could be with someone reading a selected verse or short passage aloud from as many different versions as are available. Have students summarize what it says, what it meant in the biblical context and what it means to them. Of course, the remainder of the session leads them toward the concept that has already been carefully thought out and prayerfully considered by the prepared teacher. If you choose to read from only one version, you may wish to decide which version more easily captures believers who did not read the lesson before the class. The King James Version is most popular, but it is not necessarily the easiest to understand. Making your point and moving on to the next step in the process for that week sometimes flows more easily with other versions of the Bible.

There are times when the teacher can lead believers through a sequence of questions, pausing appropriately for reflection. Such times do not necessitate believers verbalizing their answers. The teacher simply makes sure that believers go through the process of thinking. Presenting a series of carefully thought-out questions is one way a teacher can lead a class in a particular direction. The teacher insures that they go through each step outlined in the lesson of the week.

Different lessons lend themselves more to certain techniques. You can recapture images that occur while you read and study the Scripture as you design or develop your methods for delivering the lesson that week. You may think of particular music and have the CD or tape to share with the class at the appropriate point in the lesson. Individuals in the group are great resources for creativity. Think of their particular characteristics or skills while you prepare. You can call a person during the week and ask them to do something specific for a couple of minutes when called upon during the lesson. For example, ask two people to share an experience that addresses the theme. Or, on the other hand, ask them to bring a particular object that illustrates the lesson and give them the opportunity to explain its significance during the lesson. Explore different things to do as the Spirit gives you the image. What is one thing that you like to do and how can you incorporate it into an activity to enhance a scriptural concept? Ask the same question as you consider the gifts, abilities, hobbies, etc., of your class.

Choosing Appropriate Resources

To develop a concept from Scripture, use electronic databases (computer programs) and search for key words. Some that I have used include Libronix, Bible Works and iLumina. Topics that are spiritually identified for your teaching can be cross-referenced in this

Motivate

manner for a meaningful and in-depth study. Computer programs are relatively simple to use and some are available in public libraries at no cost. Simply go online. There are also a number of books shelved for your use in public libraries. There may be a seminary or school of theology in your area; utilize that library, but realize that you may not be able to borrow materials over night. Plan to spend a couple of hours browsing these resources.

Motivating Teachers and Learners

I believe that people want to be taught. "Help me to study the Word of God so that I gain knowledge of God's will for my life." This statement could be the cry of a student or leader. I asked myself what motivates me to read the Word and study to teach it. My first answer was that I want Jesus to be pleased with me. I actually like reading the Bible and I get pumped up as I prepare to teach God's Word. It is not a laborious task that I must undertake; it is a joy. I like word studies. I truly get pleasure from journaling thoughts and rereading them weeks later to see God's pattern for working in my life. I have found that it motivates others when I share how God speaks to me. It helps them to recognize the manner in which God usually communicates with them. It is also wonderful to know that my way is not the only way. Hearing how God talks to others encourages me to be attentive to other ways He may show up for me.

Conversely, there are times when I become discouraged and have little zest for the depth of preparation that is needed to feed God's people. A poster I read once said, "No one ever said teaching is going to be easy." What do I do to power up again? The last time that happened, I asked the people in my class what they needed from me. I felt confident in the relationships that had been established to solicit the help I needed from those who would benefit from the boost I needed. I asked them to tell me how they learn best and what approach I needed to take for the lessons. During a class session, I let them know that I was becoming a little frustrated and I needed them to help me to know how to plan for them. The result was that they answered me. Someone said that they needed something like a study guide with questions they could answer. Another stated they enjoyed the existing format and admitted that they were not investing the needed time. A commitment was made to do better. Still others wanted a better understanding of the connections between the Old and New Testaments, blood relationships between and among biblical characters (genealogy), and to continue allowing discussions of the concepts in the lesson.

None of their responses were new. They had shared them at various points before, but I needed a refresher. The Holy Spirit helped me to reopen myself. If I teach them every week and pray for them regularly, why can't I expose myself to them? Hearing from them was triggered a renewal of my spirit. It was like a revival. Talking to and listening to the persons in the class motivated me and reinitiated my zeal to continue the journey with them. In so many words, we recommitted ourselves to studying the Word of God together and to holding each other accountable to being prepared for class sessions. This took only a few moments before going into the scriptural lesson of the day. Subsequently, new faces began to appear in the class and the people who promised to come back, did. The regular disciples demonstrated that they were disciple makers; they shared their enthusiasm about studying the Word of God with others and the class grew from the inside out.

Teaching is indeed a gift of God. It is an honor, a privilege and a joy. What drives your teaching? Discover what motivates you. What role do others play in motivating you to be that way? How would you define the relationship that you have with your class or your staff? Take a closer look at what may set them aglow. How do you teach a Bible lesson that assists others with spiritual growth? How do you motivate others to want to learn more about God?

Motivating Learners

You can expose biblical truths in such a way that the door

Motivate

opens for learners. You can give them opportunities to explore their thoughts in connection with what the Scripture says about particular issues. You can allow them to have experiences with others, sharing how God has manifested Himself in their lives. In other words, Christian educators must be intentional about allowing believers of the Bible to participate in discussions about particular issues they have experienced as reflected by specific biblical accounts of similar circumstances. However, you can only do so much; the individual has to make the decision that it is time to grow. A Christian educator inspires others of any age to want to learn more by acting as a conduit to conversion experiences. To be a conduit to conversion, you must know your role as a facilitator. You are like a means of expression for them. You are God's instrument through which the Holy Spirit passes to activate a desire in students to want more of God and godly things. The activities, images, discussions, etc., that are shared in classes act as change agents. Students apply the concepts to their lives and can make decisions that draw them toward God's will. Illustrations make a difference—age-appropriate visual aids that make concepts portable for participants. Facilitators motivate believers to live what they are learning about.

Once a person has made the decision to follow Christ and seeks the knowledge of God's Word, the teacher serves as an activator who facilitates experiences with the Word. The experiences must be student-centered. The facilitator shows how certain passages have helped others and gives witness to what Jesus has done personally for them: "If He did it for me, He'll do it for you." The teacher does not have to do all the sharing. Learners are impelled to share their stories and become participants in their life-long spiritual journeys. Remember to utilize various modalities of learning discussed in the *Stimulate* chapter. There are so many ways to make the lesson portable.

The teacher, the conduit, is the medium through which the Holy Spirit conveys messages from God. God speaks through every participant; however, the responsibility of transmitting the message in the class setting rests with the teacher. The Christian educator serves as a temporary communicator for the Lord, who conducts a learner through the canals of life. You conduct them until they feel the power surge and connect themselves to the power source on a continual basis. When a learner becomes the carrier, the teacher knows that motivation has taken place. However, the Christian educator and the learner cannot stop there, for it is a never-ending process. You become co-laborers who not only motivate each other, but spread the Good News to still others. We need to spur each other to continue in the faith.

How do you urge someone to want to grow in Christ? You cannot, but God can. The Holy Spirit is a marvelous friend. When we depend on Him to guide us, we can do all things that lead to a closer walk with the Master Teacher. How did Jesus reach people for the Father? He started where they were and showed them truth and love. There is no law against sharing the truth. Galatians 5:22–25 tells us that, if we belong to Christ, our ungodly desires and passions have been crucified and we bear the fruit of the Spirit, against which there is no law. The apostle Paul motivated people to live and walk in the Spirit. Christian educators today can create an atmosphere that compels Christian growth. Make them want to know more by showing them the truth and believing that they can have a transformed and victorious life with the Lord. Be authentic and experience real joy. Learn how to exercise your spiritual gift and appreciate the spiritual fruit. Deliver the Word of God to learners so that they mature spiritually and do not remain dependent on the teacher.

You may be in a nighttime experience in your teaching, but know that joy comes in the morning. Motivate learners by remaining self-motivated.

Motivating Teachers

Addressing the needs of others is an important focus but it is also important to develop yourself. Teachers need motivation, too.

Motivate

Teacher training is an ongoing process. "You teach others—why don't you teach yourselves?" asks the Good News Bible in Romans 2:19–21. If you are indeed sure that you are someone else's guide, why not position yourself to be fed? Attend Bible studies offered in your church where you are not the teacher. Regularly attend conferences, workshops or seminars in your region where you can feed from the fellowship of persons in another context who do what you do and experience similar realities. There are conferences for leaders you can attend and literature you can read on spiritual leadership. Request your pastor to provide information regarding opportunities for growth. As a leader, develop relationships with leaders in other churches. Pool your resources for a broader scope.

Why wouldn't the local church routinely hold such events and encourage attendance in other places by sponsoring its members? The church should give financial support when possible. In all professions, the employer provides some form of professional development or training. Why shouldn't the church be the sponsor of opportunities for willing workers to grow?

The Minister or Director of Christian Education or the Sunday School superintendent should keep a record of those who participate and find out why others do not participate. Use their responses to restructure what is being done in the workers' meetings so that their needs are met. It does not benefit the Lord for countless hours of planning to be spent if the needs of the teachers are not met. Develop a user-friendly technique with the staff just as each staff member creates a nurturing atmosphere for his or her class. Soon afterward, hold them accountable. Where there is no accountability, there is often apathy. A church with teachers who are indifferent, lethargic and lazy generally experiences classes with boring lessons and poor attendance. Inconsistency and irregularity are other byproducts of little to no accountability. Who is motivating whom? None of this is pleasing to God.

Teachers' needs must be met. Seminars or workshops for teachers should be designed to meet specific areas of concern. The desires of the leader should be rooted in providing support for the staff, based on Christian principles. Vainglory has no place here; there is little fruit harvested in a field that is not cultivated. Focus the agenda on what will assist those who attend rather than what makes your job easier. Spend the time with the persons present and avoid conversation about who should have come, but did not. Provide a balance of topics to address what needs to be developed using various modalities as expected in the classrooms. Modeling the behavior you expect is motivational for others.

Training and Assessing Workers

Some method of evaluation should also be used for the teaching ministry of the church. Develop a forum to review a needs assessment. Then, take the time to make the most of the information or feedback received. Leaders need to keep their fingers on the pulse of the willing workers to keep them motivated as they seek to continually motivate their students. Picture the teacher as a team captain. The class represents the team. The captain is responsible for preparing the team or making (teaching) disciples. The teacher is a part of the team, a disciple who is developing other disciples. Because the disciples are effectively motivated, they become disciple makers themselves. The Minister or Director of Christian Education serves as a coach. Coaches are responsible for preparing all the disciples, including themselves.

How do you assess disciple making? Look for the fruit. It is acceptable to God to hold people accountable for what they do in Jesus' name. John 15:8 says that you show yourselves to be disciples by how much fruit you bear. The successes of teachers can be shared during a time of testimony about the teaching-learning process at regular teachers' meetings. Here is an opportunity to be proactive. Role-play issues. However, be sure to focus more on the *solution* than the problem.

Do not be discouraged or disheartened by a low number of persons in attendance at training sessions. Work effectively with

Motivate

those who are present. Some things addressed need to be handled in small groups. When something needs to be corrected, address it. If two agree concerning what they ask, it will be done for them by God because where two or three are gathered together in Jesus' name, He is in the midst of them (Matthew 18:15–20). Don't be overly concerned about low attendance. Take full advantage of it. If you really want more to come, literally feed them at least once a quarter. We do like to eat together. Every meeting does not have to have a rigid agenda.

On the other hand, if your numbers are 15 or more, some of the sessions could be broken down into small groups of 2–3 for more sharing time from each participant, then come back as a full group for closure comments. Model approaches to teaching by using them as formats for the meetings. Teachers of the same age ranges can be grouped together for one approach, but separated for another. Decide the approach according to what you are trying to achieve. If you want a weaker teacher to hear how a stronger teacher handles a particular part of a lesson, design a grouping that will put them together. Other combinations might be according to age, use of technology or other visuals, planning, writing a lesson outline, getting students involved, etc. Who is best at doing what? Give them opportunities to share at the meetings.

Dynamic lessons take time to plan and teachers' meetings could highlight techniques for the lessons as well as the exegesis (interpretation, clarification, definition and word studies) of the text. Take the time to read various things on the topic or issue before class so that there is a fresh perspective to share. Some of the lessons that we think are interesting and exciting are boring. They may have been developed with the needs or experiences of the teacher as the driving force. They may have been used before, but are not relevant to the current group. Or, the teacher may have been a lazy, last minute preparer. It is difficult to motivate someone to do something that you are not willing to do yourself.

"Help me to study the Word to show myself approved by

Reach Me With SMILES

Jesus." If your church has not had regular teachers' meetings or it has been a few years since you have had them, the following ideas may help you stoke the fire.

Training Suggestion 1 *(60–90 minutes)*

Prayer and praise — *10 minutes*

Questionnaire/Survey — *10 minutes*
Take the time to design questions that you really want to have answered.

Introductions *(1 minute or less each)* — *15 minutes*
Attendees share something in particular that others may not know about them, such as: place of birth, hobby, collector of something, etc.

Topic: What Scripture Says About Teaching and Training — *15 minutes*

Topic: Where Do We Go from Here? — *15 minutes*
Record responses for later use (flip chart, poster-size post-it paper, etc.)

Prayer and dismissal — *5 minutes*

Training Session Suggestion 2 *(60–90 minutes)*

Prayer and praise

Topic: Problems/Solutions — *15 minutes*
Role Play Issues - Focus more on *solutions* than problems

Topic: Prioritizing and Implementing: Where Must I start? — *30 minutes*

- Develop a strategy or a function of the specific groups of persons according what they do: teachers of certain age groups, secretaries, fellowship leaders, prayer leaders, etc.
- Agree upon a time and place for monthly or quarterly sharing—brainstorming, pooling of resources, combined training with other churches, networking with leaders, departments, teachers, secretaries, etc.

Motivate

Topic: Look at the Literature 15 minutes
   Read something ahead of time so that there is always a fresh perspective to share at the gatherings.
Evaluation, prayer, dismissal 15 minutes

Other Sessions

A. Meeting Purpose: Prayer
Meet together for an hour of prayer. Each person participates.
   - Read a passage from the Bible
   - Lift concerns of the teaching ministry separately, workers, students, leaders
   - Have nothing but prayer for the gathering

B. Meeting Purpose: Fellowship
   - Bonding or specific celebration.
   - Affirm one another.
   - No agenda.

Practice

Use the following passages to help you remember why you are a Christian educator.

John 14:1–13	Jesus has prepared a place for us.
John 14:14–19	Jesus will not leave us as orphans.
John 16:13–14	The Spirit guides you into all the truth.
Acts 2	The Holy Spirit came
Romans 1:1–7	Bondservant of Christ
Romans 8:16, 28	Does your spirit line up?
2 Timothy 1:5–9	Are you sincere?
Ephesians 3:20, 21	*(Meditate on this verse.)*

Reach Me With SMILES

Summary
- Training teachers is an ongoing process.
- Conferences, workshops or seminars should be held routinely and attendance at such events sponsored in other places should be encouraged.
- Support should be given by the church, when possible.
- Addressing the needs of others is as important as developing yourself.
- Restructure workers' meetings to meet specific needs.
- Evaluate and self-assess continually to motivate believers, teachers and learners.
- Be proactive by taking advantage of effective training, regardless of attendance.

Involve

How do you teach a Bible lesson that will assist believers with spiritual growth? Reach them with involvement. Give them opportunities to share, participate or implement their ideas with varied teaching techniques. Allow believers to take part in choosing the activity. Occasionally letting students tell you what they want to do keeps you fresh and free from burnout. A wealth of information and ideas can be found when you take the time to look for it. It could be right before your very eyes.

Teaching to Transform

We have done some things effectively in our teaching for some time now. How long have you taught in the church? Think of how society has changed within that time. Did the context of your teaching ministry change? Does your style reflect the way you were taught or the way you taught when you started years ago? Now may be the time that a transformation takes place within your mind so that the Master Teacher measures your teaching strategies.

Transformation implies that a change is in order. What does the change involve? There is a literal change in form. The structure that has been used is modified. Transformed teaching is the result of a teacher cutting across their standard procedures and making different connections with the students and the Word of God. Therefore, another change is personal. The teacher develops the desire to be different, to teach differently, to use different approaches.

When we are transformed, our methods need to change. We ask students to grow in the Lord and we look for evidence of that spiritual growth. Do the people who attend church with us see growth in us? Has our lack of methodological transformation stunted personal growth and student growth? Could there be more student-centered teaching and involvement with Jesus as the model for both teacher and student? Just as students need to hear a Word from the Lord, the Christian educator does, too. How often do you hear from God while teaching? The Holy Spirit can move in your preparation as well as during your delivery.

God wants His people to be delivered from the things that separate us from Him. Being stuck in practices that worked previously, but no longer work, can stunt the effects of teaching now. There are times when we should resort to tried and true methods. However, there are times when there is something better. What is the Lord saying today about how He wants the lesson on a familiar passage to be taught for today's believers? Sometimes teachers who have been teaching for a while need to reconnect to the source and purpose of Christian teaching. That reconnection is a transformation. Rethink how you teach and why you teach and transform your style. Modify approaches to accommodate the passage being taught. Let the Scripture guide the method. We often attend workshops and find cute activities and approaches. We transport them to our context before considering whether they are appropriate to the scriptural text. There is a time and place for everything, but keep it in the perspective of using the best method for the concept lifted for the specific scriptural lesson. There is an appointed time for everything. And there is a time for every event under heaven—

Involve

A time to give birth, and a time to die;
A time to plant, and a time to uproot what is planted.
A time to kill, and a time to heal;
A time to tear down, and a time to build up.
—Ecclesiastes 3:1–3

Are you a seasonal teacher? This year you are the king or queen of the overhead transparency. Next, you use the videocassette for everything. Before you know it, you are overusing the computer and the LCD projector to "powerpoint" pictures, outlines, notes, and anything else you can imagine. Do you pick up trends in teaching for the sake of the trend? Current technology is everywhere. I often use it in teaching; however, sometimes the mechanism distracts the message and the nature of the lesson being student-centered is lost. Use technology as it directly fosters the involvement of the learners. A Powerpoint presentation could be three slides not thirty—just enough to arrest the attention, capture the image, provoke discussion or delineate steps in a process. Not every lesson is the right season for certain technology (or whatever trendy method is in vogue).

Are you the kind of seasonal teacher who overuses trends or the type who chances to seize teachable moments? Teachable moments seem to appear out of anything at anytime. They are those times that you didn't plan to delve into an illustration or point, but the opportunity is right there. You could not have planned it, but you can seize the moment because your lesson is well-prepared. It is so easy to just describe the scene or event because it boomeranged where the students were mentally engaged at the time. There is a season of opportunity for every learner to be reached. Everyone is savable and everyone is teachable.

There are so many possible teaching seasons to consider for everyone involved. In season and out of season, always base the lesson on the Scripture. However, how will you know if it is the season to build the students or chastise them? Is it a season for new faces or the same old faces week after week? Is it the season of a hot moral issue or social debate? For any age group, what season is it? How can you use the season to involve the students? Would you use the same type of fertilizer for houseplants, lawns and crops? Surely, you recognize the need to diversify instruction to reach all who come. Is it time to change your type of fertilizer? Your crop may be in need of a different formula because an immune deficiency has occurred. You no longer see the effects you think you should see. Look at yourself before placing blame anywhere else. Maybe growth is stunted because the appropriate "fertilizer" is lacking. The student is in the growing season and the teacher is disconnected. The student is budding and the teacher is sitting in a disengaged state. The student is emerging and the teacher is detached. Perhaps the teacher does not recognize that she is somewhere else and needs to mentally relocate and transform some methods. Is the teacher trying to force the whole group to conform to a standard that is no longer viable?

> *It is hard to explain, since you have become dull of hearing. For though by this time you ought to be teachers, you have need again for someone to teach you the elementary principles of the oracles of God, and you have come to need milk and not solid food.*
> —Hebrews 5:11–12 (NASB)

How do you teach a Bible lesson that will assist believers with spiritual growth? Change your standard teaching method from season to season and allow students to be actively involved in their Christian education as a requirement in various stages of the teaching-learning process. Involve all learners regardless of age.

> *Test yourselves to see if you are in the faith; examine yourselves! Or do you not recognize this about yourselves, that Jesus Christ is in you—unless indeed you fail the test? But I trust that you will realize that we ourselves do not fail the test.*
> 2 Corinthians 13:5, 6 (NASB)

Involve

Since Christ is in you, He is the model. Jesus did not use only one method to reach people to whom He ministered; however, He allowed their involvement in the process. He engaged them. When direct involvement in the teaching-learning process is a two-way street, more learning takes place. Transformative teaching is teaching that changes form or structure based on one standard, the Bible. Transformative teaching is teaching that has Jesus as the model for the believer, for both teacher and student alike. Transformative teaching reaches people where they are and brings about deliverance, hence transfiguration.

Teaching for Transfiguration

Transfiguration is a type of reformation that is another type of restructuring; it is forming again or rethinking. A different framework results from a metamorphosis that occurs for the teacher and student as they share God's truths in holistic ways. Using these strategies should become part of a perpetual process. Using this method yields more effective, life-altering, transfigurative teaching; stimulate, motivate, and involve believers in the process of teaching and learning. How can this be implemented?

With the intention of reaching the people of God for their spiritual growth, the teacher must be receptive to spiritual food for personal growth. Transfiguration is personal. The first consideration is the teacher as the learner. After God has revealed Himself to you through the Holy Spirit, He will work through you to reach others in the way that they need to be reached. Do you see the role of the teacher as tantamount to being a spiritual leader in the church? As a spiritual leader, you accept responsibility for the sheep in your pasture (class). *"Be on guard for yourselves and for all the flock, among which the Holy Spirit has made you overseers ...* (Acts 20:28). Granted, the pastor is overseer of the whole flock. When you accept the responsibility of teaching in the church, you are agreeing to assist with the nurture of some of the sheep. It is after you have sat with the Word and let it permeate your own heart that you will have a heart to hear how to transmit the message of the lesson to someone else.

> *You yourself are a guide to the blind, a light to those who are in darkness, a corrector of the foolish, a teacher of the immature, having in the Law the embodiment of knowledge and of the truth, you therefore, who teach another, do you not teach yourself?*
> Romans 2:19–21

Yes, teaching is an awesome responsibility. It is a gift of the Holy Spirit; the same Spirit empowers you and allows you to do what you do. Why not involve the sheep as often as possible and as much as possible? Their involvement becomes your barometer of effectiveness. Plan to take advantage of everything they offer to the teaching-learning process. More than one person will receive the message from the Scripture, therefore use a variety of techniques and approaches for your lessons. No one method will work effectively all the time. Consider the key concept and context of the lesson, then meditate on how God wants you to deliver it to the understanding of others. How does a particular person in your group learn best? Modality is simply the method by which they perceive and understand. Fashion the facts to fit the face of the learners for the lesson in front of you. That kind of interpretation facilitates application of the lesson. Less time will have to be spent in class reading the Scripture and more time can be used for developing and applying the concepts. Believers will be more likely to read before class because they know that they will be given an opportunity to make the Scripture fit their particular situations in life.

Consequently, learners are the second most important feature in lesson preparation. No, I am not overlooking the importance of the presence of God's truth; the content is the base on which the teacher and the student stand regardless of the dominant teaching-learning style. One person is verbal, but another person is more auditory. On the other hand, Sister Let-Me-See-It is visual, while Brother Let-Me-Do-It is kinesthetic. It is not so important that the

Involve

teacher has this way or that style of teaching. The important thing becomes removing yourself so that others are reached for Christ by any means necessary and available.

How will the lesson provide for spiritual transfiguration? Consider the context of biblical transfiguration. Everybody will not be able to see it but they will hear it and believe. Jesus told all of the disciples of His suffering, death and coming glory. Six days later He took three of them to the mount of transfiguration where they saw His face shine like the sun. They saw Moses and Elijah talking with Jesus. All of the disciples were not able to see the transformation that revealed His future glory. Jesus told the three when it would be appropriate for the others to hear of it (Matthew 16:27–17:8; Mark 9:1–10).

Has anyone seen Jesus while you were teaching? Is it possible today? How will the lesson provide for the spiritual transfiguration of you and the believers?

Practice

Read the following items with self-reflection. Pray for God to block out others, so that you can focus on you.

1. Read the text devotionally, apart from reading it to study.
2. Observe what the Scripture says.
3. Interpret what it means to you.
4. Apply how it relates to your situation in life.
5. Later, list methods of presentation that capture the context and concept.
6. REACH the student! Teach them to read the passages of Scripture for themselves, observe what it says, interpret what it means and apply how it relates to them today.

—continued

7. Go to the session expecting that they will begin to read at home daily during the week and show them by example how that enriches your life.
8. After the lesson has been taught, take the time to evaluate it.
   a. How did the lesson provide for spiritual transfiguration?
   b. What is the effect of using your gift of teaching?
   c. How does your gift affect your relationships?

Jesus did not approach His life and ministry haphazardly. His mission was far too important. He gave His best; He gave His all. His approach and method were appropriate for the time, setting and people to whom He related. As a result, people characterized His teaching as new, authoritative and different from the teaching they heard from others. In John 13:12–15 Jesus told them to do as He had done. Jesus modeled His message and used a variety of approaches. He used parables (stories), objects, drama, discussion, questions and answers, and lecture. He was innovative; He taught anytime and anyplace, with the resources on hand. Teaching with Jesus as the model means teaching a message clearly for spiritual transformation (Johnston and Brown, 2000) and transfiguration.

To summarize, transfigurative teaching is sort of like structural renovation; it is crossing the former lesson outline to reach a different view. Embracing a framework that is unusual for you results from a metamorphosis, a change for the teacher and student from the inside outward.

Points to Ponder

Spend a period of meditation considering transformation and transfiguration in the Bible.

—*continued*

Involve

1. What is the point surrounding each of these two verses? Consider the verses that precede and follow each in the Bible.

Romans 12:2 _____

_____

Corinthians 3:18 _____

_____

2. What does each of these passages have in common?
    Matthew 17:2–13
    Mark 9:2–13
    Luke 9:28–36

_____

_____

3. How are they different? _____

_____

4. How can the similarities and differences be applied to teaching today? _____

_____

5. How is John 1:14 similar to the three passages above?

_____

_____

6. Distinguish between transformation and transfiguration.

_____

_____

Reach Me With SMILES

Setting Goals and Objectives

Specific objectives and goals must be measurable. Objectives are statements that describe the specific action that is desired as the result of a specific lesson. The objective, then, is something that can be observed by others; it can be seen and not just heard. The objective defines a specific action that demonstrates that the goal has been achieved. Goals are broader biblical concepts that emerge from the lessons that are to be applied to the life of the believer. The teacher and the student should be able to determine whether the goals and objectives are being met. For example, a believer is able to forgive a relative for something that happened years ago. The believer shows mercy after participating in a lesson from Matthew 5:7; 23:23 or Romans 5:8.

Develop a guiding purpose statement for the lesson that is based directly on the Scripture at hand. Glean the statement from a passage or a single verse. Design everything in the lesson that day to uplift the concept in the statement. It will guide all activities and the development of questions toward a particular purpose. Justice, mercy and faith are weightier matters of the law, but the lesson's focus is mercy. A comparison or contrast can be made among them, but the emphasis is to develop only one of the three, mercy. Because of a more thorough investigation of mercy, a believer may choose to alter something about their life that reflects a choice to change. That is a measurable behavior. What can a person do to show mercy? They may not only say they forgive because of the conviction from being justified by faith, but also treat the forgiven individual differently. The believer will be able to show forgiveness as a measurable objective under the broader goal to discuss various aspects of mercy.

In addition, setting specific goals and objectives helps keep the Christian educator focused on the purpose of Christian teaching. Jesus Christ is the source of Christian teaching. Christian teachers teach to develop lives for Christ; the ultimate goal of reconciliation and relationship with God must be imbedded in each lesson. Therefore, the Christian educator must move from non-evangelistic

Involve

lesson outlines toward a "new people coming in" mentality. Each lesson must reach others for Jesus today. The believers will walk out with the Word this week and be compelled to share it with others.

The activities selected for the lesson should reflect the complexity of learning styles of the persons present and consequently involve most of them. When the purpose of the teaching moment is clear to the teacher and procedures are implemented that focus on the one aim, measurable results can be evidenced. Believers will share testimonies of experiences with God or personal evangelism. Because of a specific act of forgiveness, not only does God bless the one who forgave, but also the person being forgiven. The persons who observe the dynamics of the revitalized relationship are affected as well. Lifestyle changes will be evident as seen in demeanor, conversation and ministry involvement when testimonies are shared. Set up a class atmosphere that intentionally facilitates sharing, which will be a method of measuring the goals and objectives.

To facilitate improved teacher performance we must prepare ourselves in the Word by doing the same three things we want the lessons to bring out of the believers: observe what it says, interpret what it says, and apply what it says. Then we can set a goal based on the reading. Read the Scripture in different versions to observe what the message is from the Holy Spirit. Use the version that is easiest for you to understand for general reading and rereading (King James, New King James, New American Standard, New International, Good News, etc.). Read it to feel it. Later, as you study, observe every word and how each word is placed in each sentence in a certain order; observe how the verse would be different if a particular word were not there. Though you read different versions and different words, one goal of the verse will become apparent for your edification and later for your teaching. Then, write down the nuances within one version or changes you observed as you compare other versions. Interpret what it says and apply it to your own life and experiences before planning to teach. As you study the Bible make sure that you take the time to observe the context then interpret what the Word says. Do not be to quick to jump to application because you may have missed a nuance that is the life-altering hinge.

Improving personal performance prepares you to involve students more effectively. Perhaps you have not read anything in this process that is a new thought for you. That's great! This gives you an opportunity to unclutter something that lies within you. Retrace your steps. Possibly you have piled on so much over the years that you have forgotten who you are and why you teach. Getting rid of the clutter releases you to recognize a kind of self-separation, dividing one part of who you are from another. You can begin to reprioritize those parts. As your journey of rediscovery continues, approach application for teaching once more. What are you supposed to do as a disciple, trainer or nurturer, and how do you get it done? Discipleship, discipleship training and nurturing are all processes, too. Where are you as a disciple?

There has to be a goal or an intentional purpose for what you do as a teacher that points others toward Christ. A goal is something that you want to achieve that can be measured. Stop and think for a moment about a lesson that had an impact on you. There was a specific aim that targeted you as a believer in order for the teacher's mission or objective for the day to be accomplished. (I am assuming that you not only teach but make it a priority to be taught.) What was the objective or goal of that lesson? You might say understanding the Word or learning to depend on God more.

Now think about what you will be teaching next. Let's ask the same question differently. What are the achievements that you anticipate as a result of teaching this lesson? How many ways can you say the same thing as you reinforce that one message? The answers may be communicating with God, listening to His Word, obedience, positive attitudes, etc. As a result of teaching these specific lessons, what achievements do you anticipate? How will you know that believers have achieved the goal or how can you measure what believers achieve? How will you know that someone learned obedi-

Involve

ence? You might say that believers could apply it to their daily lives, through their testimony, walk or actions. It is good for a believer to know the broad or general goals of bringing others to Christ and meeting Jesus face to face one day. It is also necessary to know that in the meantime, or as we tarry day by day, "What will I do with myself? Today, I need to work on being obedient."

How does a teacher get this point across? Answers to that question come when you are studying. Specifically, how do you work on being obedient? The answer should be located in the Scripture lesson, unless you pulled something that was not in that particular passage and you need to reread it. Coming up with "obedience" and "listening to God" is what you receive in your spirit as a teacher while you are reading. Remember that reading and studying are two different steps: yourself in relation to the Lord (what the Bible says and what the Holy Spirit tells you about you at the time you read it), then yourself in relation to other people. Always know that Jesus is who holds things together.

If your Bible teaching is for a particular purpose ask the question that will lead you to where you are trying to go. Use as many methods or activities as time will allow, repeating the same objective to ensure that the main point is made. Some people are more gifted with the ability to think on their feet and ask poignant questions, while others need to exert more effort and energy. One is not better than the other; each is equally effective. Most things can be taught if a person is willing to learn. If you need more practice with asking the right questions to achieve the desired effect, consider the stem of the question. Look at the first few words of a question. For basic facts use the type of question that requires lower level thinking. Who? What? Where? When? These help you to get started, but do not load your lesson with these because they are prone to keeping the believers at a lower level of spiritual maturity. You want to grow people. Deal with issues. Ask open-ended questions where any answer is acceptable. These questions may include the following:

"In your opinion..."
"What you would do if ..."
"Have you ever been faced with..."
"Has there been a time when..."
"Would you like to share a time when..."
"What did the verse say to you..."
"How does it speak to your life..."

    Teachers need to understand the process of learning to be a disciple or follower of Jesus. In addition, teachers need to understand discipleship training as a process to recognize which stage they are working on at a particular time with each individual. Therefore, we would be in a better position to know on which part of the process a particular lesson should focus. The Holy Spirit provides this wisdom; we need to know to ask for it as we prepare. Our students need to know that we care about them enough to systematically plan toward specific objectives and goals, if we are going to be effective. Believers may not want to sit in a class with someone who is not willing to show himself and share experiences as the Holy Spirit relates all of it to the Scripture at hand. Teachers become facilitators of a faith walk with Jesus. Become the expert of the process of learning about the Lord and share the benefits to bless those who sojourn as co-laborers in Christ.

    General goals, objectives and specific achievements are the things at work here. How do you write the exact achievement that believers will be able to demonstrate as a direct result of participating in this lesson? If they get only one point, what is that point, Lord? Be very intentional about writing down a statement that represents the one thing that believers will take with them as a result of the next lesson that you teach. Take a moment and ponder that point now.

    Always take a moment for reflection in your reading, study and preparation for teaching. If you need to process your thoughts

Involve

as you prepare, believers probably need to process as they receive messages in a learning environment that is conducive for the Holy Spirit to move. Slow down, sometimes, for a few seconds of reflection.

Improving Preparation Techniques

- Set a teaching objective or goal based on your personal time with the Word. If you were teaching, what would be the goal? Process the concept of the verse. Identify the concept in order to write a single statement.
- Isolate key words in order to help you focus on a teaching point or specific goal. Choose words that would be non-offensive to persons in your group rather than "trigger words" that produce negative images. For example, some versions use "master" as opposed to "teacher." Depending on the depth of a person's ethnicity, an issue of authority may come up in a person's mind that takes them in a different direction. You do not perceive it until they ask something or make a statement that leaves you wondering, "How did they get that out of what I said?" Lead with "teacher" and later substitute "master" as you go and the word "master" will be understood as "teacher"; you intentionally take people from where they are to where you want them to go. (The assumption here is that you continually take the time to build relationships and that you know the people that comprise your class. Even when there is a new individual or visitor present build in time for sharing that makes everyone comfortable and gives you an opportunity to begin to know them from the beginning of the class session.)
- Discern words that may cause trouble because you are person-minded. Make sure that your terminology helps you to connect to where believers are. Do not avoid issues; simply be aware of how you address them.
- Choose words that are authentic for you, not outside of your

personality. Don't be too colloquial, if that's not you. Do not intentionally use words that are outside of who you are in an effort to reach others, especially youth. Keep it real because people know when you are not and you may be perceived as phony.

- Does each version use the same key words?
- Distinguish teaching points from broader concepts. Stay focused under the leadership of the Holy Spirit rather than diverging to every specific detail at an inappropriate moment.
- Consider the context. For example, you cannot deal with John 13:13 in isolation; you must go back at least to John 13:1–12. Also, under consideration must be chapters 1–12 and whether or not there is a chapter 14; what does it say in connection to the others. Then, you might be in a position to share the fruit of your study with somebody else.
- Come up with questions against the Scripture. Challenge the Scripture by asking it questions. Use terminology to be people friendly but not out of your character. Move people from where they are to where you want them to go as a result of what you know you are trying to achieve—the concept, goal, objective.
- Effective teaching depends on your ability to make it relevant and keep it real. By the time people walk out of the teaching session, what is it that you really want them to have in their hearts? Jesus is Lord and teacher.
- Asking questions does not necessarily mean that people are going to walk out with the answer that leads to the concept of the day. Keep focused on the one point that they will leave with. Regardless of the length or liveliness of discussions that may arise during the course of the session, what do they need to know?
- Raise a question that will be relevant to the everyday life of your group. It does not need to be a factual question. Come

Involve

up with something that believers need to wrestle with, at least a little bit, so that it can penetrate deep within their spirit. Who was the Master Teacher? Was Jesus the Master Teacher? Believers may silently beg you to feed them more than the obvious. How is the Lord the teacher in your life? Why do I need Jesus to teach me anything? To what extent is Jesus the master in your life? Why is Jesus considered the greatest teacher?

- Phrase the question in a way that the listener is clear on what is being asked. If the question is too long, the hearer may not know your intent. You may need to break the longer thoughts into smaller pieces that assist you in leading to the ultimate question. Put the thought into a capsule so that you are sure to get to where you want to go.
- Now, identify the one statement for the Scripture you are about to teach. The statement of purpose should not be too long. Eventually you will be coming up with activities to support it; hence brevity keeps the teacher as preparer focused.
- Too many important concepts within one purpose statement makes the process of choosing activities confusing and possibly frustrating due to time constraints.
- Build a brief sentence from which other statements, questions or activities can be developed. The person may clearly understand what the teacher said ought to be true from the Christian's perspective. For example, "I understand the teacher said I should acknowledge Jesus as my teacher." Whether believers confess within their hearts that Jesus is their teacher is another matter. The concept has to be clearly taught before the student can walk out with a message for God to increase within them.

Reach Me With SMILES

Points to Ponder

- Know yourself. Intentionally establish positive relationships with the people that you lead (your class) on a continuing basis. How are we going to teach people if we do not take time to get to know them?
- Share your self. How do you include what you like to do in your ministry of teaching for Christ without continual lecture and soapbox?
- Apply what you receive from the Word. How does that biblical message connect to my life? Then explore "How can I teach it?"
- Effective objectives or goals must be measurable. What are the achievements that you anticipate as a result of teaching this lesson?
- Don't give an overload of information. Keep It Simple, Saints (a Holy KISS)
- One important thing in this process is to know where you are trying to go and using appropriate terminology to get you there without losing anybody. When you sense that someone is not where you are in thought for whatever the reason, the teacher is responsible for pausing to make sure things are cleared up. It may be a facial expression or other body language. Keep them involved.
- Be aware of making assumptions as you lead discussions. One could assume that they are considering the Lord as their teacher. Your saying it does not make it so. People make choices daily and we need to acknowledge free will daily.
- When teaching, be sure to give students some think time to ponder the question. Let the room be silent before rush-

—continued

Involve

ing to call on someone or to give a personal discourse. The questions should connect to the people in the class rather than to the teacher per se. Does the "you" in your questioning force students to look at themselves or their teacher? You want the Word to penetrate their hearts. Be careful that the attention is pointing away from the teacher as the center; the connection is to be made that relates to the individuals present so that they can walk out with it, use it and share that message with others for Christ.

- Remember that the passages we read in the Bible had one original meaning with multiple applications. You can more effectively teach one at a time. Reading the Bible daily and studying it are two different things; effective teachers do both. Read every word in context recognizing that the use of a word changes over the centuries. In addition, you must follow a process as you spiritually prepare yourself, then prepare to teach. You must observe, interpret and apply the scriptural text. The more you apply this process and the more you teach, the more you should grow and be able to help others grow in the Lord.

Practice

Repeat the process again. Remember the importance of repetition, as you want the believers to mimic biblical lessons in their lives to bring them closer to Christ. Observe, interpret, and apply Ezekiel 36:26–28.

Reach Me With SMILES

Summary

You are sitting at home reading the Bible. Then you are studying the Bible. Now let us pretend that class is in session and you are concluding the lesson. The purpose statement is like jumping so far ahead in lesson preparation that you are at the end of the process. So we ask, "What is the point of this passage?" Once you know what you have received from the Holy Spirit through meditating with different versions of the same passage, you have the point or the concept. At this time you are ready to consider methods, procedures and other questions that can be used to fill in the remainder of the lesson. Spend the most time in lesson preparation, absorbing the Word in a personal way. Do you know who you are? Are you meditating on the Word personally? Is your preparation for teaching being guided by what you think you are going to get out of the process of teaching? "What is the point?"

The controlling factor after your spirit has been fed needs to be feeding God's sheep. The brief purpose statement along with a lesson title can control your thinking. As you focus on the specific message that will feed someone, acknowledge the place of the Holy Spirit. Ultimately, they may be drawn closer to the Lord. The teacher spiritually transforms so that he or she facilitates the believer's transfiguration. Lifestyles change as the teacher and student draw closer to God.

Further Reading

Johnston, Jay and Ronald Brown. *Teaching the Jesus Way: Building a Transformational Teaching Ministry*. Nashville: LifeWay Press, 2000.

Love

How do you teach a Bible lesson that will assist believers with spiritual growth? Christian educators should Stimulate, Motivate, Involve and Love each of the sheep entrusted to them. We have expounded upon a variety of approaches to reach students; we now turn to a very basic tenet of the Christian faith: reaching learners with love. Once the atmosphere is set for stimulating discoveries of the Word, your students are compelled to participate, and you are so personally prepared that their involvement is evident, do not neglect basic demonstrations of loving them.

You might ask, "How many ways can I show or tell my students that I love them?" Show love according to John 15:12–14:

> *This is My commandment, that you love one another, just as I have loved you. Greater love has no one than this, that one lay down his life for his friends. You are My friends, if you do what I command you.*

How does Jesus' love feel to you? How does it feel to be Jesus' friend? We must overtly demonstrate that we love the people before us. You have to feel that you do. You must know that you do. Many times in Deuteronomy the people of God were admonished to love Him. Their love was shown through specific acts of sacrifice, offering, worship, and being in good relationship with one another. The commandment that Jesus gives us does not offer us a choice, if we want to be His friend. We *must* love one another. How should you show yourself friendly in a teaching-learning environment? The same way you do anywhere else. It becomes part of your personality as a Christian. Though you compartmentalize yourself when studying the Word of God to determine what facet of your character God is addressing at the time, you are one person. Your personality is either loving or it is not. Be aware of yourself; what you do or say that turns people off or on. How does your personality show love? How can you generate an authentic loving atmosphere? What do you do to make your students *feel* Jesus the way you do when you know that He loves you? Pursue love (1 Corinthians 14:1). Be intentional about following after love.

Demonstrating Love

Roman Christians showed their love for Paul by being present for him. Their sacrifice was made to go the distance, literally, to get to him (Acts 28:15). The apostle used the word "charity" in 1 Corinthians 13:1 to explain what love might look like. Charity is described as the greatest of the three Christian graces: faith, hope and charity (1Corinthians 12:31–13:1–13).

Love is more than a display of intellect, which was worshiped in the days of Paul. When your teaching becomes mostly "heady," love reconnects the learner to the lesson. Do not resound like brass. Your ability to understand deep mysteries or your abiding faith and knowledge about the Word of God are nothing if the participants do not sense that you love them. Show your love by what you give to them with patience and kindness. Avoid the appearance of being boastful envious, rude, or seeking your own glory. Be aware of how you react to things your students say. Do not show that you are annoyed or angry about their contributions to the class. Show that you value them, what they say, and what they do. That is what love looks like.

Christian educators fulfill part of the Great Commission—making disciples. We are doing "whatsoever" Jesus commanded. Believers who come to us are saying, "Reach me by loving me." After self-reflection, you might be spiritually ready to lovingly lead others to a closer relationship with Christ. That's the heart of Christian discipline.

I have conducted several workshops and seminars where the question came up about discipline in a church classroom. Colossians 3:12–17 speaks of what we should do. Since we are the elect of God, we should put on what looks like God. We must bear one another and forgive one another. Christ forgives us! When we let the peace of God rule in our hearts, the product is love, even when believers are not behaving in a manner that we agree with at a particular time. *"Let the word of Christ dwell in you richly in all wisdom, teaching and admonishing one another."*

Applying Discipline in Love

Why should we discuss discipline in this context? All learners need to know that you care enough to invest the time it takes to understand them. We need to give attention to this in our churches as we train our teachers. How do you teach a Bible lesson that enhances spiritual transfiguration? Love me by leading me. Lead me by teaching me how to apply the Word of God to every aspect of my life. Lead me by loving me with accountability for my actions, comments, and thoughts. Sometimes problems handling discipline stem from personal perceptions, self-confidence, or relationships from the teacher, the student, or both. As you continue to read, understand that discipline applies to any age group, children, youth, young adults, and older adults alike.

What is discipline? We can mean different things when we say discipline and those who hear us may think something totally different. For example, Webster's dictionary gives these among other definitions of discipline: a field of study; training that corrects, molds, or perfects; punishment; control gained by obedience or training; orderly conduct; a system of rules governing conduct. There is also a set of verbs that describe the actions of people who discipline: punish; train or develop by instruction and exercise; bring under control; impose order upon. Which of these do you mean when you speak of discipline?

From my studies in college to become a Special Education teacher, I learned that discipline could be negative or positive. Negative discipline generally renders some form of punishment for undesirable behavior. Goals are set and a program of activities or plan of action is developed that leads toward that goal. Positive discipline on the other hand refers to a planned series of activities or exercises considered necessary for the attainment of a certain goal. This positive training would include routine activities with things that are allowed and other things that are restricted. Generally, this describes the way we function on any job without a lot of overall complaint because we sense the need for some structure. In school, a curriculum leads to a certificate, a diploma or a degree. For an athlete, intensive training can lead to winning. A mechanic's apprenticeship may someday lead to managing or owning a shop. Generally, a set of rules must be adhered to for adequate positive discipline to be maintained. What would the community be without guidelines for practicing law or medicine? The implication for the Christian educator is that there are guidelines the church must follow and they are found in the Bible. A practicing Christian must exercise positive discipline in fear of God, who will punish or reward when eternity comes.

Another way of viewing discipline is with the thought that one person or authority limits the behavior of another. If the person in authority over a group is not imposing the boundaries, a spectator may think, "They need discipline." Perhaps that carefully prepared part of the lesson was structured as a lively rather than quiet activity. It is evident that there are different perspectives regarding

Love

what discipline is and what should be done about it. Regardless of which definition you use for a particular situation, there are implications for strategies that may be helpful to effectively and lovingly handle discipline in a Christian classroom. There are as many disciplinary styles as there are perspectives on discipline. Punishment is the most prevalent style used to change undesirable behavior. Suppose God punished me for every indiscretion on my part? Woe is me! If the teacher dictates discipline, it is centered around giving the teacher an expected outcome. That outcome is usually based on the teacher's perception of the behavior and the action toward changing it. Task-imposed discipline is limited to what is needed for that particular activity or event. The group commands another style of discipline; the majority of the persons involved participates in the discipline process. Although there may be a place for each of these, self-imposed discipline is the goal toward which the Christian educator should strive. The disciplinee ultimately learns the biblical basis for godly character and an inward change manifests itself outwardly that others know that Jesus is in the heart. The teacher and the group are observers of each other, all learning and growing through the grace of God. That mission is possible. It is a process that will take time, but it is attainable with patience.

There are also many methods and techniques of discipline. Arrange the learning environment to avoid difficulties and undesirable situations. This means that the teachers who plan only one day in advance must change (transform) the way they prepare to teach. Time must be spent in prayerful meditation so that the Holy Spirit can deliver the plan of action to you. Who knows what the disciplinee is going to do, except Almighty God? Seek to hear first from the Father through the Son so that the Spirit can advise you. This may not happen if you can only squeeze in a few hours the day before you enter the learning arena. You would not be entering as the champion or the victor because you have set yourself up with the uncertainty of an incomplete plan for the people of God. The need for proper planning is affected neither by the age of believers nor whether they are male, female, or a mixed group. Disciplinary problems in any classroom can be curtailed by more effective planning, with the aid of the Holy Spirit. The loving Christian educator views problems as opportunities for God to use her to begin creating something new for God.

When problems arise that you would categorize under the umbrella of discipline, restructure the learning environment in some way; it does not have to be drastic. Stay focused on the message of the day. Ask an open-ended question that has been planned into the lesson to redirect attention to the Word of God. The Holy Spirit has given you the direction for the lesson. (Your pastor or Director of Christian education may have assisted.) The enemy wants to take the focus away from God. That is not acceptable. A Christian educator may view her role as a disturbance or confusion reducer. God is not the author of confusion. This implies that we must particularly plan for circumstances that would thwart the delivery of the message of the day. If you know that a disciplinee often talks out of turn, use that knowledge to the benefit of the lesson. Plan questions or at least one activity to intentionally draw that person into discussion designed by the Scripture you are teaching. Let that person assist you in implementing the activity. Let him lead at least one of several small groups to answer a probing question. This way, more people have an opportunity to share, rather than having one person monopolize the center stage. Have the groups come back together and their spokespersons present their conclusions. The participants are required to demonstrate love through mutual respect as each delivers their contribution.

Let God help you to set the stage. Create opportunities for your students to experience God with minimal anxiety each time they come into your learning environment. Making enough time for proper planning is a key factor. When distressing situations do arise, the question becomes, "Holy Spirit, how do I redirect their attention to God?" When you have planned well, you are not an anxiety producer; you have confidence in what you have been given to present.

Love

You also have confidence that the Spirit of God will indeed give you the words and the behavior for that very moment. Your response could be simple body language. For example, slowly move close to a disruptive individual as you continue the procedures for the lesson. They know what they are doing is annoying (or down right aggravating) and your proximity calms them. Perhaps they just want attention. Give them positive attention. All that is needed, in some instances, is a physical change in your location in the room, accompanied by a gentle smile, with no words to address them. Continue the lesson. Do you believe in the God that you teach? Teach like you believe so that believers experience how you summon the assistance of the Holy One.

Appeal to the conscience of the disciplinee. A nod, a hand on their shoulder, or any other gesture that does not interfere with the learning environment may be all that is needed. If you make an emotional response that sounds or feels like a verbal assault, impatience, or a desire to be anywhere but near that person, your witness to them and the other students is weakened. Those most damaged may be the observers rather than the disciplinee. If we equate discipline with maturity, we will see some similarities. People who are immature do not necessarily consider the result or the consequences of their actions beforehand or afterwards. They operate from the perspective of what they want and where they currently exist. In contrast, a spiritually mature person's conscience would be pricked to know that something they did or said caused an adverse reaction in someone else. As Christian educators, we must make attempts to move a person from not caring what others think to caring that the environment was negatively affected as a result of something they said or did. Again, this does not refer to any specific age group; any class has an enrollment of persons with different levels of social and spiritual maturity. It is not the problem; it is an opportunity for God to be seen.

Another disciplinary method or technique gives disciplinees less attention for undesirable behavior than may have been given previously. Sometimes they are starving for attention and have used negative behaviors to get any attention they can. In order to get the attention they desire, require a disciplinee to exhibit desirable behaviors. Either way, as a Christian educator, you are Christ's emissary or ambassador. We cannot afford to handle discipline in the same manner that may have created the undesirable behavior in the first place. We are Jesus' agents for changing hearts, rather than making aggressors more aggressive. If your disciplinary concern is, "They won't let the teacher teach," consider that you may be talking too much. What is teaching to you? From the previous sections we learn that teaching is more than one person speaking prepared information to a quiet, attentive group of listeners. Sometimes they are listeners, but there are other facets to the learners.

Add a few more open-ended questions to stir up the curiosity of the group. Use questions or statements that will cause them to question each other, then give them an opportunity to discuss the topic (minus your voice) for a few minutes. The ultimate goal of your teaching is to provide opportunities for believers to experience God in order to make life-altering decisions. A more Christ-like change in lifestyle can stem from participation in discussions or activities that are not contingent upon the teacher. Changing your role from *teacher* to *facilitator*, from time to time, enables changes to take place in your students' behavior. Their involvement in the lessons produces lasting impressions that can be replicated when they face life's challenges, long after leaving the session. Isn't that what we want? In order to get a handle on the discipline issue, we may first need to get a handle on ourselves—the way we prepare for a lesson and the signals we portray as we deliver it. *Be a tension reducer, not a stress inducer.* **Do not provoke. Do not nag.**

How can Christian educators teach and impose discipline? The people who come to our churches (including us) are the same people who make up society. Therefore, implications can be taken from that context and effectively used to glorify the Kingdom of God, since God has made information available to us. If some Christian

Love

educators feel that they cannot be effective because one or two believers are not "disciplined," what are they to do? One approach is to take a look at what discipline is, then see what Scripture says about it. None of this will mean anything without applying it to the contemporary situation that raised the initial question.

The idea here is to look at the implications that arise from society as a whole, "society" loosely meaning gathered groups of people. Once we perceive the context of individuals exhibiting undesired behavior, we have a better understanding of who they are. Christian educators teach discipline by going back to the Bible to find out how Jesus Christ taught it, then by taking believers to the Bible to show them where the Bible speaks of specifics for their context. This requires that the teacher have a personal relationship with Christ and a sense of self-disciplined study with an active prayer life. From these come love, peace, and patience (longsuffering), which are fruit of the Spirit.

I am reminded of a group of male participants in the Summer Enhancement Ministry at my church. One particular day one of them began to call himself a Pharisee. The ministry was a day camp, so we were together all day. From time to time, I noticed that he was gathering more followers who would chant, "Pharisee, Pharisee, Pharisee." It sounded like members of a sorority, fraternity, or gang chanting the name of their group. It became a distraction, which they thought was amusing. I eventually got them together as a group during a break and asked what made them start that, directing the question to the ringleader. He very arrogantly let me know that it was in the Bible. I gave them a homework assignment to find the word *Pharisee* in the Bible as many times as they could, then read for the situations and tell me the next day who the Pharisees were. The behavior the next day was remarkably different. When I asked halfway through the day, "What's a Pharisee?" the ringleader was the first to say, "I don't want to be one of them. Them guys was against Jesus."

In other words, lovingly deal with unruliness or a student may

Reach Me With SMILES

run into the arms of the enemy because of your reaction to their misbehavior. If you cannot deal with a particular situation because it is it too hard, get help from a mentor, a seasoned saint. Brainstorm some strategies that others in your area have used to overcome the same type of problems you face. Your answer may be found in a person within or outside of your church family. Attend local workshops and ask the questions that you need to have answered. When you do that in the Spirit of the Lord, God points you to the person with the word for you. Trust the Gospel that you teach, or stop teaching! When high expectations are maintained and modeled by the leaders, the followers will be more orderly. Accountability is crucial.

Help believers to develop emotional maturity for self-discipline. It has to start somewhere and there may not be anyone in the home modeling the behavior you think is appropriate. The child, the parent, and the grandparent may exhibit the same behavior. Do not be judgmental, focus on the soul being won for the Lord, discover the strengths of the individual, then use them for God's glory. Show students, whatever their age, how to praise the Lord for the gifts that have been freely given. Lovingly point out where Scripture says this gift that they take for granted is an anointing from God, created in them for God's purpose. In Jeremiah 29:11 we are reminded that God knows the plans or the thoughts that He has for each of us, for good, not for evil. *Show troubled believers the Word of God.* Remember that everyone is savable, and these individuals are in your class for a reason. Refrain from beating them over the head with the Bible; use it with meekness, gentleness, peace, patience, and love.

How do you teach a Bible lesson that will assist believers with spiritual growth? *S*timulate, *M*otivate, *I*nvolve and *L*ove them. Reach them with love. How do you teach a Bible lesson that enhances spiritual transfiguration? A metamorphosis can occur for both the teacher and student as they share God's truths in holistic ways. Help others develop self-discipline as you develop a variety of techniques

Love

that reflect the love of Jesus through your actions and the Word of God. The enormity of the discipline factor diminishes when you are secure in the gift of teaching that the Spirit has given you and keep an open mind to learn from believers. Using disciplinary strategies should become part of a perpetual process. Using this method can yield positive disciplinary results. How? Self-discipline can lead to self-love. Are you limiting behaviors in others because you need limits in your own behaviors? Many who are unprepared to teach have spiritually confused those wanting to learn. "If I could get them to be better than me…" Change that approach. Ask God how He wants you to lovingly *lead* the process of spiritual growth. How can we lead where we are afraid to go?

Students say, "Reach me by loving me." But, how can they accept your kind of love, when they cannot see that you love yourself? Students say, "I see God's love, for He wakes me up. I know Jesus loves me because He died for my sins. I accept the love of the Holy Spirit, who indwells me." But the way they see you handling circumstances in your life makes them question whether the end (eternity) justifies the means (their choice and yours to continue this Christian journey). What happened to you that caused you to not love yourself? What can students do to avoid being a spiritual mess?

Points to Ponder

Jesus calls us to action-oriented teaching ministries; God calls us to do His will. These come by way of spiritual self-discipline that precedes our efforts to lovingly lead others to follow Christ.
- Develop spiritual discipline for yourself continuously.
- Discipline yourself to study daily.
- Dare to see yourself while studying.

—continued

> - Do not retreat, but use available resources to move to the next level of personal growth and development, whatever that is for you.
> - Learn to understand yourself and increase your love (acceptance) of yourself. After self-reflection, you may be spiritually ready to lovingly lead others to a closer relationship with Christ. That's the heart of Christian discipline.

This is a handbook for developing disciple makers. You have read this far because you are a disciple who wants to assist other disciples to grow in their relationship with the Lord. A disciple is a disciplined person. When you develop disciple makers, you are teaching Bible lessons and behaviors that you practice yourself. Others see growth in you and believe they can grow also.

Dividing the Word Rightly

Habits are routine behaviors practiced and developed over time. Jesus' disciples learned and practiced under His tutelage over a period of time. They "submitted to Jesus' discipline, they aimed through obedience to resemble Him, as indeed He invited them to do" (Ryken, et.al. 1998). Jesus once said, *"A pupil is not above his teacher; but everyone, after he has been fully trained, will be like his teacher"* (Luke 6:40).

"Reach me with love that looks like you have Jesus' joy or I am going to find another teacher!" Will your students' next teacher be in the church house, crack house, or the nip joint? The people of God are really no different than any other gathered group of people. We help make up our society, with all of its problems, and we bring the whole package with us to church; we are all sinners saved by God's grace. Christian educators and church leaders, what you say is important and what you do is important. You are responsible and accountable to God for how you divide His Word (2 Timothy 2:15). God's people are learning from what they see and hear from you.

Love

However, we must keep in mind that you cannot be responsible for their choices. Christian educators must be obedient to the Word of God. We must be true to the content of our teaching; we must rightly divide the Word of truth. When we stray from the Word, we are vulnerable to consuming the bait of God's enemy. The bait is anything that separates us from the love of God and our ability to impart the Word of truth for Christ. How can we fish for men (Matthew 4:19) if we are not focused on the Father? Lift up the name of Jesus, even in the midst of what you deem to be negative behavior, and He will draw all unto Himself.

We sometimes develop a slave mentality. We chain ourselves to a particular structure, tradition, format, or just wanting so much to get through the material. We want to do what we want to do so badly we forget that we have prepared the material to get through to the people of God. If students do not hear the truth being taught in an age-appropriate manner, all kinds of problems may arise while we are teaching. These problems may appear at ages from children through senior adults. Rightly, or appropriately divide the Word so that the Spirit of God can do His job of convicting the spirit of man, woman, boy, or girl. When teachers have problems understanding how to maintain discipline in their classrooms, they should immediately secure the Holy Scriptures. Monthly, in my local church, we read our church covenant. It includes a part that says, "We further engage to "… cultivate Christian courtesy; to be slow to give or take offense, but always ready for reconciliation, being mindful of the rules of the Saviour in the eighteenth chapter of Matthew, to secure it without delay…" (*The New National Baptist Hymnal* 1974). When we seriously accept that we are in covenant relationships, the way we demonstrate love is transformed. The routine becomes seeking the best responses and reactions according to the biblical mandate, which never changes.

Christian educators cannot afford to be easily angered by what some call "discipline problems" in the Christian classroom. *Let every man be swift to hear, slow to speak, slow to wrath for the wrath of man does not produce the righteousness of God* (James 1:19, 20). This refers us to hearing and doing the Word of God as examples or ambassadors, even in the classroom. The way we react and respond may be the very image of godliness believers see that causes a cataclysmic change or life-altering decision to follow Christ Jesus as personal Lord and Savior. James goes on to say that we must be doers of the Word, and not hearers only, deceiving ourselves. Not one of us is beyond the need for heeding these words. We cannot forget what we are really like as well as what we used to be like. Someone modeled Christianity enough that we became followers. Routinely exercise the spiritual fruit of patience, peace, and love, while God does what is needed in the lives of believers

Leading through Love

Teachers are leaders who need to be led by spiritually focused superintendents, pastors, and regional leaders. How do you teach a Bible lesson that will assist believers with spiritual growth? Love them enough to lead them by example. Many feelings and emotions arise when we talk about leadership that loves and how things ought to go. Each person has his or her own opinion, based on something or other. But, when it comes to expressing thoughts, awkwardness sometimes appears. Teachers should be able to hold their leaders accountable, just as students should be able to hold the teachers accountable to being Christ-like examples.

One way to keep your finger on the pulse of the group is through informal but written assessments to gather information. Surveys are one way to get raw information and real answers to questions you really want answered. Envision getting all that information in writing so it can be examined. How do you implement the ideas gleaned? It is important to take the time to think through what the participants have said in order to follow through meaningfully and effectively. Part of the process is to do something with the results, or don't bother to solicit the information. The most important part of asking the right questions is listening and showing the

Love

people that you care about or value what they have to say (See Appendix C).

Conducting a survey produces a great source of information. However, some congregations have been overly surveyed. They are constantly asked for ideas and information, but little is done with the data collected. Following a survey, it is important to compile the information for the participants. They need to have a picture of what the survey implied and what will be done about the implications. In addition, be deliberate about finding ways to put into practice something as a direct result of the survey. If it was important enough to take the time to start the process, it is important enough to follow through. How valuable is simply having information? This could be the springboard for your next session or for personal study and spiritual growth.

Points to Ponder

The Scriptures below will help you to stay rooted in your purpose.

Mark 10:35–44	-	to serve
Philippians 2:5–8	-	with humility
I Peter 4:7–10	-	with servant love

Practice

Show love first in your home.
Show love everywhere you go.

Further Reading

Ryken, Leland et. al., gen. ed. *Dictionary of Biblical Imagery.* Downers Grove, Illinois:, InterVarsity Press, 1998.

The New National Baptist Hymnal. Nashville: National Baptist Publishing Board, 1974.

Encourage

How do you teach a Bible lesson that will assist believers with spiritual growth? The teacher should Stimulate, Motivate, Involve, Love, Encourage and Strengthen all believers. Believers who come to us are saying, "Reach me by encouraging me." When a person becomes an active participant in a local congregation, their journey is beginning, not ending. The care, time, and concern shown as the Word is presented to them must be continued. Someone, somewhere invited them to your place of worship or to your class. How do you keep them? You must SMILE: Stimulate, Motivate, Involve, Love, and Encourage them. You cannot help them grow if you cannot keep them encouraged.

When Barnabas arrived in Antioch and saw the evidence of the grace of God, he encouraged the people (Acts 11:22–23). The writer of Hebrews reminded his audience of their confidence in Christ, the hope they professed, and the need to exhort or to encourage one another toward love (10:19–25). Whatever keeps you involved and motivated may be the key to keeping others encouraged. Develop new strategies for retaining people. Look introspectively for answers to the following questions to assist you in this part

of your growth and development:
> *What keeps you involved in the church?*
> *What makes you want to quit sometimes?*
> *What can be done to prevent you from wanting to quit sometimes?*
> *Who is responsible for preventing you from dropping out?*
> *Why do we want the church to grow?*

(See Appendix C)

Teaching in Diversity

Teaching is a spiritual gift (Romans 12:6–8; 1 Corinthians 12:28–30). That gift assists Christians with making disciples of others who have accepted Christ as their personal Lord and Savior. It helps Christians explain the Gospel to others in order for them to make the decision to accept Jesus. Teaching is the spiritual gift that enables one to "study God's Word and to communicate spiritual truths in such a way that they are relevant to the health and ministry of the church and in a way that others will learn" (Garner and Martin 1995). Webster's Dictionary gives several definitions of the verb *teach*: to cause to know a subject; to cause to know how; to accustom to some action or attitude; to make to know the disagreeable consequences of some action; to guide; to impart knowledge; to seek to make known and accepted.

Diversity is the condition of being different or having differences. People are innately different from one another. Being diverse means we are unlike each other and have various forms or qualities. This is Webster's way of defining diversity. Additionally, a Christian should define it as a necessity and characteristic of the church where Jesus Christ is the head. Though more than one person in a particular body of believers may have the same spiritual gift, the "gift-mix" (McCalep 1999) of individuals within the body provides opportunities to minister to the needs of the entire body. Scripture says that there are diversities of gifts given to the body of believers in Jesus; one of those gifts is teaching.

Christian educators must see teaching through the lens of the

Encourage

Holy Bible. Jesus *taught* the multitude many things (Mark 6:34). Barnabas and Saul *taught* in the early church (Acts 11:25–26). In Colossians 2:6–7, people who had received Christ were being admonished to walk in Him, being rooted firmly, built up in Him, and established in faith, just as they had been *instructed*. The term in these passages comes from the Greek word *didasko* which means to instruct by word of mouth; to influence the understanding of the person who is taught; as instruction in the Christian faith and teaching. The same form of this word is found in Romans 12:7 and Hebrews 5:12.

God appointed teachers in the church (1 Corinthians 12:28). Since this statement appears amidst the discussion of the gifts of the spirit for the common good of the body, we know that we should have persons teaching whom the Holy Spirit gifts for that ministry. Are people who are not gifted to teach by the Holy Spirit teaching the Word of God in our churches ? We should not become so diverse in our local churches that we continue to allow this to be. Our educational ministries must not continue to function in our churches differently from what is mandated in God's Word. Corinthians 12:4 tells us that there are varieties of gifts but one Spirit. Verse eleven says that the Holy Spirit is the One who distributes (divides or classifies) those gifts individually as the Spirit wills. Those who have the spiritual gift of teaching must be the teachers in our churches.

We must look at the teachers on our staffs and hold them accountable for recognizing whether or not they are gifted by the Holy Spirit to teach. The fact that a person teaches in the school system or conducts training programs for their profession does not necessarily make them the best pick for a teacher of the Word of God. While it is true that such persons can use their abilities in the name of Jesus, we must select teachers with giftedness as the priority. (I want to remind you that I have secular teacher training. I am not bashing schoolteachers; I want to emphasize that a professional teacher and a gifted teacher may not be one in the same.)

Reach Me With SMILES

We must also look at learners as a diverse group and become person-minded in our teaching. Diversity in the body of Christ is a part of the description of the body. We must recognize the importance of our differences and teach to the differences assembled in the learning environments God allows us to provide. (Review the chapters entitled *Stimulate* and *Motivate*.) The Spirit of God gives unity to the body; we are not trying to teach everyone the same way, nor should we look upon each other as though all are the same. Scripture confirms that we were created to be spiritually different for the common good of the fellowship of believers of which we are a part.

Encouragement must be a vital part of the lessons we impart as Christian teachers. Knowing our subject or curriculum is not enough; encouragement is affirming others in their walk with the Lord. Christians give encouragement to show that they value and appreciate the worth of another individual. How do you teach a Bible lesson that will assist believers with spiritual growth? Assure them that they have the ability and the spiritual capacity to use their God-given gifts to enlighten the corner of the world in which they reside. Everyone cannot identify with everyone else. However, individuals speak to the needs of certain persons because they reflect something familiar. God made us in His image and gifted us so that we glorify Him. Within the context of our experiences, we minister to the needs of others that God places along our path. He gives us what we need in order to speak truth to those we encounter. The Holy Spirit is a gift from God that we receive when we become born again believers in Jesus Christ. The Holy Spirit deposits within us a special gift from God that is to be used to edify others for the uplifting of the Kingdom of God. Each Christian is gifted in a particular way for his local congregation for the work of that congregation in meeting the needs of their community (Ephesians 4:11–12).

We need to refresh our teaching strategies to include the reality of the diversity of believers in the body of Christ. We can take comfort in knowing that God joins the members of the body

Encourage

together and can revitalize us as we accept, affirm, and encourage others to be their authentic selves in Christ.

There is beauty in the diversity of the body of believers in the Lord Jesus Christ. When we preach and teach God's truth, the Gospel of Jesus Christ, the Lord adds to the church. At that point, persons need to be discipled; they need to be taught the Word of God for righteous living. This teaching needs to be in the context or in the reality of who the persons are or who they have been created by God to be as defined by their giftedness. We must make disciples by helping people discover and use their spiritual gifts.

Using Gifts for Disciple Making

One of the roles of the teacher in making disciples is reaching people where they are and helping them to see that who they are is why God can use them. It is because of the gifts they have and the experiences they have collected that someone else will come to know the Lord. The gift helps to determine and define the method a person uses to be an effective witness. Each person is needed to reach someone else and Christian teachers need to be encouragers so that the testimony of those they teach will be vital to the growth of the church. Barnabas was sent out by the church in Jerusalem to Antioch to verify the growth of the church among the Gentiles. When he saw the grace of God, he was glad and encouraged them all that, with purpose of heart, they should continue with the Lord (Acts 11:22–23). Help others to know they have a purpose in Christ.

Discipleship can take place in any forum where the Word of God is studied. As believers mature as disciples, we must encourage them to become disciple makers. Teachers are encouragers who see the value in diversity for Kingdom building. We are responsible for equipping people to disciple others and must therefore recognize the diversity that comes with the body having many members (1 Corinthians 12). The ministry of the teacher includes embracing all and finding creative ways to reach all for Christ. It is at this point that we become teachers for spiritual transformation into the very likeness of Christ. How did Jesus teach? He knew what methods to use for each situation to convey the same message. He understood the context of His ministry; Jesus was a disciple maker who embraced diversity.

To each one of us, grace was given according to the measure or amount of Christ's gift, the Holy Spirit. The Greek term being used here for Christ (*Christos*) means *anointed* (Ephesians 4:7). In other words, being gifted means being anointed. We must acknowledge God's ability to anoint whomever He wants with the gift that He wants them to have. As a disciple maker, help others to understand that they have a measure or capacity for the gifts they have. We are gifted diversely, or differently, to equip the saints for service to build up Christ's body. The whole body is fitted together and properly joined by every member of the body. The proper working of each part causes growth (Ephesians 4:1–16). Therefore, we must encourage people to grow according to the measure of their giftedness. We must accept them as they are. Once we evangelize and bring them into our fellowship, we must help them move to the next spiritual level as we move to our next level by using our gifts as teacher/encourager. In his book, *Stir Up the Gifts*, Dr. George McCalep lists evangelism and assimilation as advantages of a gift-based ministry. We can help others to know where and how they fit into the church body. Christian educators must help others understand why gifts are given at the time of conversion and allow time for discussion of their individual gifts for the common good (1 Corinthians 12). Make time available for students to share where and how they fit into the ministry model of the local church. This will assist the fulfillment of individual callings for service in the name of Jesus.

[I am making a strong assumption that those who are reading this and serving as Christian educators in their local churches have discovered, developed, and deployed their gifts. It is unfortunate, but true, that some leaders in our churches do not have a clue what their own gifts are. For that matter, when you mention gifts, some

Encourage

leaders do not think of the spiritual gifts as listed in the Bible. As I chaired a committee at another local church, I began by surveying the strengths and weaknesses of the persons appointed by the pastor to serve. To my surprise, they listed all kinds of things as gifts they brought to the table. I handed those surveys to the pastor and chose another route of assessment. The pastor decided to revisit the teaching of gifts to the congregation though that pastor had previously addressed it.]

The question is not only whether or not we have teachers teaching who are not gifted to teach, but do we have leaders leading who have neither the gift of administration, nor the understanding of the necessity for a gift-based ministry.

Christian educators must help others to understand the need to be good stewards of gifts (1 Peter 4:10–11). Originating from the Greek word *oikonomos*, "steward" refers to a person who manages domestic affairs, as applied to the apostles, ministers of the Gospel, and private believers. As servants of our Lord Jesus, we serve by the strength that God supplies to the measure the Holy Spirit gives us individually. Teachers, then, help others to see this as a means of glorifying God through Christ. We must overcome any fear of using the gifts of God for specific ministry tasks by being a good steward of our gifts (McCalep 1999). We must also learn and teach about spiritual gifts because God does not want us to be ignorant.

Points to Ponder

Identify your spiritual gifts.

_____   _____
_____   _____

—continued

How are they being used to benefit your local congregation?
_____
_____
_____
_____

Name at least three individuals you have assisted with spiritual growth within the last six months. (Your personal relationship with them may help your assessment.)

_____   _____
_____   _____

We must teach everyone, without exclusion, so that they are presented complete before Christ (Colossians 1:28). Become true disciples so that what follows is disciple making.

Practice

What will you do within the next three months to demonstrate your commitment to being an effective disciple maker? How will you:

Stimulate	_____
Motivate	_____
Involve	_____
Love	_____
Encourage	_____

Further Reading

Garner, Larry and Tony Martin, *Gifts of Grace: Discovering and Using Your Spiritual Gifts*. Jackson, Mississippi: Baptist Books, 1995.

Encourage

McCalep, George. *Stir Up the Gifts*. Lithonia, Georgia: Orman Press, 1999.

Johnston, Jay and Ronald Brown. *Teaching the Jesus Way: Building a Transformational Teaching Ministry*. Nashville: LifeWay Press, 2000. Zodhiates, Spiros, ed. The Hebrew-Greek Key Study Bible.

Strengthen

The final aspect of the SMILES concept reminds us that our approach toward Christian teaching has to be theological. The theoretical foundation must comprise a belief system that is rooted in Christian convictions evolving out of your personal experience with the Lord. The Christian approach to teaching establishes a base for each lesson that is derived from self-directed and continual personal study. Self-evaluation or self-examination is expected; recognize yourself and see whether you are in the faith (2 Corinthians 13:5). Can you say, "I recognize that I am a part of Christ because He lives in me"? When Jesus lives in you daily and you continue to prepare to teach others, you know that you Stimulate, Motivate, Involve, Love, Encourage and Strengthen others. How do you teach a Bible lesson that will assist believers with spiritual growth? Believers come to us saying, "Reach me by strengthening me." Know that one of your roles is to edify the body of believers. Ephesians 4:11–16 tells us that Christ gave some to be teachers so that they could prepare God's people for service. In order to serve Christ, we must be edified, built up, and strengthened. We must become mature Christians ourselves and then assist others in attaining the measure of the fullness of Christ. This reminds me of safety instructions reviewed before any airline takes flight, "Be sure to secure your oxygen mask *before* assisting others."

Each of us must continue to grow in God's grace in the unity of the Holy Spirit joined together and held together by Christ, the Head of the body of believers. As we build up others who grow and mature in the Word, they learn to build up still others who grow. Thus, each person does his or her part according to the spirit that works within. We must be open; we must be willing to discover, uncover, and recover all that keeps us pointed in Christ's direction. We must not cover ourselves up with anything except the banner of Jesus. We find in Christ the strength that helps us to reach others for Christ. People on a faith quest will recognize the Spirit that lives inside and be drawn to Him. They will not be drawn to you, but to the Christ that lives within you. Then we become obligated to edify learners or strengthen them for the remainder of their Christian journey. The lessons we plan to teach should strengthen our students for life's journey. The spiritual maturity level for students in any class is diverse. When you finish your lesson, will believers be able to see and feel the Lord in it? Will those who are yet uncertain be drawn closer to a heartfelt decision for Christ? If they are, you have strengthened them.

Moving Beyond Discipleship

Discipleship is personal; it is about "me" and "my" relationship with the Lord. Disciple making takes discipleship to the next level. We have a personal relationship with the Lord as a disciple and we grow because of discipleship, the process of learning to be like Jesus. Now that we are maturing in our faith, we reproduce others who want to know Jesus and desire a closer relationship with the Father. We move from simply being a Christian to going out, searching for, and satisfying the needs of others so that they come to know who God is through Christ. That is disciple making. Disciple makers want to cultivate hearts for Christ. When we make disciples, we are

Strengthen

about building God's kingdom. So, the question is, are you growing? Are you growing spiritually? In what way is growth occurring? Are you changing and is that change moving you in the right direction—toward God?

> ## Points to Ponder
>
> Read Acts 17 and think about how Paul made disciples. Using the entire chapter, list action words that show what he did. See if a pattern emerges. [Note, 16:37 lets us know Paul is included in "they." Start with verse 1.]
>
> _____   _____
> _____   _____
> _____   _____
> _____   _____

Making Disciples

The word *disciple* is used once in the Old Testament and more than 200 times in the New Testament (Matthew, Mark, Luke, John, Acts, I Corinthians, Galatians).

And many among them shall stumble;
They shall fall and be broken,
Be snared and taken…
Bind up the testimony,
Seal the law among my disciples. —Isaiah 8:16

The phrase "make disciples" is used once in the Bible.

"Go therefore and make disciples of all the nations teaching them to observe all that I commanded you; and lo, I am with you always, even to the end of the age." —Matthew 28:19–20

Reach Me With SMILES

What is a disciple? A disciple is a follower, a learner, a student. What is discipleship? Discipleship is the process of learning to be a follower of Jesus Christ. It involves building a personal relationship with Jesus and requires time studying the Word of God, praying to God, and exercising your spiritual gifts.

What is a disciple maker? A disciple maker is one who teaches others the things that Jesus commanded and how to observe them. How do you make disciples? Teach them! Teach them to observe the things commanded by God. Disciples share the Word of God and produce fruit. An apple tree produces apples. A pear tree produces pears. A fig tree produces figs. A disciple maker produces other disciples. Disciple makers help others to see their need to be in a growing relationship with God.

> "Abide in Me, and I in you. As the branch cannot bear fruit of itself, unless it abides in the vine, so neither can you, unless you abide in Me. I am the vine, you are the branches; he who abides in Me, and I in him, he bears much fruit; for apart from Me you can do nothing. If anyone does not abide in Me, he is thrown away as a branch, and dries up; and they gather them, and cast them into the fire, and they are burned. If you abide in Me, and My words abide in you, ask whatever you wish, and it shall be done for you. By this is My Father glorified, that you bear much fruit, and so prove to be My disciples."
>
> —John 15:4–8

What is the difference between discipleship and disciple making? Discipleship is personal and occurs when an individual has decided to follow a model or particular set of beliefs. Disciple making involves teaching others. It happens when an individual is intentional about helping others to not only choose to be a follower, but also grow. Disciple making is a process that begins with a plan. We must count the cost, which includes time, energy, and emotional involvement. Then, we must proceed with edification and strengthening the body of believers. Jesus said, "Upon this rock I will build my church" (Matthew 16:18). Each Christian is a rock upon which the church (universal) has been built. Read and study the Bible to grow closer to God. Disciple making takes discipleship to the next level. When we make disciples, we are about building God's kingdom. We have a personal relationship with the Lord as a disciple and we grow because of discipleship, the process of learning to be like Jesus. Humbly and peacefully accept the Word of God when you read it, especially when it makes you feel awkward and uncomfortable. I agree with a statement that I read in *First Steps to Understanding Your Bible* by James M. Gray, that we must not be too proud to learn or to obey what we read, although such obedience may be difficult at times. Receive the Word planted as a seed put in fertile soil that will gently sprout. Let the Word blossom in you because it will save you when you let it grow.

Strategizing for Disciple Making

Effective Christian educators understand and accept that the task of teaching is not all about themselves. This is not the place for you to be self-absorbed. Romans 12:3 reminds us not to think too highly of ourselves, but have sound judgment. Good judgment helps our prayers revolve around others rather than self. What *we* want is not the focus. Matthew 5:6—*Hunger and thirst after righteousness and be blessed.*

- Don't be angry or despondent when you don't get what you expect. It doesn't get to be about you.
- Don't lose heart, for your inner man is renewed daily while the outer man decays (2 Corinthians 4:16–18).
- Don't fear failure or criticism. Our adequacy comes from God (2 Corinthians 3:5).
- Your highest aim should not be self-fulfillment. When you lose your life for Jesus, you save it (Luke 9:24).
- The Ultimate Goal: How does this glorify God?
- Ask, How does my ministry involvement glorify God? Does

it minister to the Lord? Does it minister to the saint? Does it minister to the sinner? Does it conquer Satan and his kingdom?

Increasing Teacher Effectiveness

Sometimes problems do arise in the area of staffing. The nature of volunteerism, untrained and non-gifted teachers, and inadequate curriculum can become thorns in the flesh of the Christian educator. Volunteers are not always dedicated to making long-term commitments. Therefore, specifying short-term appointments (13 weeks, one year) might help. The short term could be for a regular class or a special emphasis topic. When the person sees that the responsibility terminates at a designated time, the commitment could become firm. You know when the term expires, which gives you time to explore the next step: the same teacher, another teacher, or another topic. The opportunity is built in for the volunteers to rededicate themselves at the end of that year or use the gifts they have in another area of Christian ministry. That phase becomes a growth tool for personal development and discovery. The church benefits when its members recognize whether or not God has called them to work in specific areas.

Untrained teachers may become frustrated. They may feel that the curriculum is inadequate or burn out before becoming equipped. Spiritual mentors can be helpful. One person becomes available to assist in a new teacher's development. Being able to ask questions, discuss ideas, and air reasons for frustration are important parts of growth. Mentor someone in an effort to edify and affirm him or her. Strengthening them strengthens the students. As you share teaching techniques, you both grow. Position yourself so that you bear fruit that is portable; you can take it wherever you go. Imagine the effect on believers as they learn by observing this process of sharing. After all, we are commanded to go and tell others. We are not supposed to keep what God has given us to ourselves. By reaching one, we reach others.

Strengthen

Increasing your own effectiveness is a byproduct of helping others, but it also presents challenges. The first challenge is to know yourself. Who are you and what is it that you like to do? Hold on to that thought. I challenge you to come up with a way that God can use it. Although your first thought may not be a religious thing per se, God can still use it. If God gets the glory out of it, then it can benefit God's Kingdom. How do you use what you like to do effectively for the ministry of Christ? Each person must authentically work with the gifts they possess together with the gifts of others to benefit the Kingdom. Nothing is a small thing; the gift is what you are to do in the name of the Lord. Think of how the best artisans were told to create a certain thing in making the tent of meeting and religious paraphernalia in Exodus. God told Moses exactly what to make, how to make it, and whom to choose to make it. One was best at working with fabric, another gold, wood, etc. What is it that you truly like to do? How can you use it for the ministry of Christ? When you poll your staff in search of their answers to such questions, service projects promoted by the education ministry emerge. Different classes or groups develop project ideas that fit their gifts. A person to coordinate the education ministry projects will also emerge. People using skills and gifts they enjoy remain loyal longer.

Think of the last lesson you taught or the last lesson that someone taught to you. What did the main person in this lesson do? How can you look back over the past week and show a specific example of where you demonstrated that trait in your own life? Or, was there an opportunity that you missed? Daily reflections become the food for fruitfulness, a byproduct of Christian teaching. Therefore, a second challenge one encounters when trying to become more effective is personal application. The teacher can become so busy preparing to teach that the private connection of biblical messages is lost week after week. We must faithfully allow the Holy Spirit to reveal something in our lives that demonstrates His presence. Experience the difference between how you felt about the last lesson you taught and how you felt when the Spirit connected it back to you. If you are really teaching, you are trying to effectuate or facilitate a change in the believers. Use the Bible as a tool to get the Word stirred up in people, but until you use it personally, what have you done? Make sure that the Word feeds you before thinking about how it is going to feed your students.

Another challenge is to share yourself. Find someone with whom you are already comfortable, a person with whom you can share yourself within the sphere of who you are. Look at where you go every day and to whom you talk. As you avail yourself to others, God moves more mightily in your life. Discover that all of life's daily experiences become a part of teaching.

Summary

Increasing teacher effectiveness is a never-ending process. Reaching out to mentor another uncovers what people need because you are hearing them. You may need to come up with classes that have not previously existed in your church to meet the needs of the congregation. If there is not a vehicle in the church to minister to an expressed need, develop it, so that the people can be fully fed. If you are not going to respond with action, there is no need to listen. As you journey through the Bible, make it apply to your own life. Otherwise, how can you teach it?

Teacher effectiveness is a byproduct of helping others to spiritually grow and it presents challenges. As we strengthen others we must remember to strengthen ourselves and stay rooted in the Word.

We must not let our thinking deter us from obedience to the Great Commission. People need to feel that someone cares about what happens to them. They need to feel that they are wanted, that they belong, and that they are needed. Strengthen them.

Strengthen

Points to Ponder

List key ideas that are important factors for teachers.

_____
_____
_____
_____
_____
_____
_____
_____
_____
_____
_____
_____
_____
_____
_____

Now, go forth and teach "all nations."

Studying the Word of God

In order to participate in the process of being transformed into the image of Jesus Christ, Christians must study the Word of God. Ministry must be committed to the growth and development of Christians. Do you have a desire to live and keep God's Word? Is your prayer like the psalmist's who prayed, *Open my eyes, that I may behold wonderful things from Thy law* (Psalm 119:18)? Studying the Word of God to attain spiritual knowledge from God is expected. We should study the Bible with diligence, humility, and prayer.

Prayerfully enter the study of God's Word so that you hear God. Allow the Holy Spirit to be manifested. Whether you are at home, or on a break at work or at school, be intentional about how you enter the presence of the Lord. The time that you set aside to study the Bible is important. Plan time to pray before you read the Word, to prepare your heart and mind; pray while you study to insure the purity of your thoughts. Also, plan enough time to pray after you have sat with the Word so that you hear God and internalize His truths. Avoid being rushed with your study.

Here are some suggestions of ways to study God's Word: with diligence, desire, dependence and discipline. Diligence in studying the Word of God requires desire, dependence, and discipline from you. They are prerequisites to the effective and diligent Bible study of every believer. In Acts 17:11 the people of Berea received the Word with all readiness and searched the Word daily to discover truth. Our desire for God strengthens us. James 4:8 tells us that we must submit to God. When we yield to God and resist the devil, the enemy will flee from us. We must want to be in God's company. God draws near to us as we draw near to Him. We have to want to stop doing things that are not pleasing to Him. We metaphorically cleanse our hands of things we used to do because of a desire to please God. When we purify our hearts, our desires turn to wanting to know what He wants us to know and what He wants us to do. In addition, Matthew 5:6 says, *Blessed are those who hunger and thirst for righteousness for they shall be filled.*

Another prerequisite for Bible study is dependence upon the Holy Spirit. John 14:26 tells us that the Holy Spirit will teach us all things. Additionally, 1 Corinthians 2:10–13 tells us that God reveals through His Spirit the things that He has prepared for those who love Him. Since we cannot know the mind of God, we must depend on the Holy Spirit to help us understand the things of God. We have received the Spirit, who is from God, that we might know the things that have been freely given to us by God. We must study so that our speech is not man's wisdom, but God's, which the Holy Spirit teaches. There are times when being dependent strengthens us.

Therefore, discipline in applying yourself to the study of the Word is another prerequisite to diligence in studying the Bible. Paul

Strengthen

told Timothy to charge the people not to strive about words to no profit, but to be diligent to present themselves to God (2 Timothy 2:14–15). In other words, study in such a manner that will please God when you share the Word accurately with others. This way you have nothing of which to be ashamed. Discipline strengthens.

> ### Points to Ponder
>
> Read all of Psalm 119 and meditate on it. Journal your thoughts.
>
> _____
> _____
> _____
>
> Study the Bible with the kind of gratitude that makes you thankful daily just to have it and be able to share time with God. When we value something, we hold it in high esteem. Its importance can be seen in our thankfulness for having it. Our gratitude gives it a place of significance because it is worth something to us. What is the revival of the soul worth to you? The law of the Lord revives the soul and gives joy to the heart. Do you consider the Bible more precious than gold and sweeter than honey from the honeycomb (Psalm 19:10)? The reward in keeping the ordinances of God is great.

Reading the Word of God

The way we read and the way we study are not the same. Turn your attention to reading the Word of God for all its worth. When Christians read the Bible, they comprehend what the words say. When you study, the Holy Spirit is teaching you while you read.

When Christians read the Bible, they understand writings.

Reach Me With SMILES

When you study, you gain knowledge of the truths of God. When Christians read the Bible, they convert what they see into meaning by relating it to their own experiences. When you study, you scrutinize what is being said in the text.

When Christians read the Bible, they glance at the surface of words. When you study, you research and dig for deeper spiritual meanings. When Christians read the Bible, they may recite what has been said. When you study, you consider reasons why it was probably stated that way.

When Christians read the Bible, they scan for particular words to trigger something within. When you study, you carefully look at every word and wait for the Holy Spirit to speak through every nuance or fine distinction used from one text and language to another. When Christians read the Bible, they examine the words in relation to the words around it, one kind of context. When you study, you examine the passage before and after the one you have read according to the big pictures that God shows you (biblical context).

Reading requires the skills of seeing and pronouncing words in relation to a particular context. Without the context, the words have no meaning and reading does not take place; we are merely looking at the words and calling them something. We need to look and the words of Scripture and come away with what God is saying, what the passage means, and how we can use it in our lives for the glory of God for the entire world to see. Observe. Interpret. Apply. Therefore, we must improve our basic reading skills while we are reading the Word of God so that we get what God is trying to tell us.

Are you a disciple or a disciple maker? Or, are you both? As a disciple, you strengthen your individual relationship with God through Jesus Christ. As a disciple maker, you help others to learn about Jesus and you teach them to obey all that Jesus commanded (Matthew 28:19–20), while you continually strengthen your personal relationship with the Lord. Understanding this distinction will help

Strengthen

you to strengthen others in the name of Jesus.

An article entitled "Removing the Training Wheels" (Discipleship Journal, Jan/Feb 2003), raises an important question: How do you help those you are discipling to begin ministering to others? My thoughts turned to another question. How many of us are ready to move to another level in our service but won't because of insecurity or apprehension of failing?

Have you been discipled repeatedly and just cannot see how God can use you to minister to others? When you are spiritually mature enough to begin ministering to others, you see the needs of others. Keep it simple by taking small steps that you can handle, and stay connected to a spiritual mentor. I pray for opportunities for each of us to grow in our walk with God, individually and as disciples who make other disciples. While you wait for God to develop you, be faithful in prayer. Be as patient with those you disciple as God is with you. Do not give up on them. Be diligent in prayer and be available as an instrument of God. God will deliver you and God will discipline you; these two things work together to develop us into disciples that will be focused on the Father. He wants us to be so committed to Him that we fulfill the Great Commission of Christ. "Go and make disciples."

However, before you can make a disciple, you have to be one. If you are seeking self-gratification and glorification through what you do and say, get ready to be disciplined. In studying the book of Isaiah, I was struck by God's promise to preserve the survivors of the Assyrian and Babylonian exiles who honored and praised Him. Isaiah wanted to know how long he would have to prophesy to God's people. He was purposely sent on a mission to a people who would not listen. God told him to prophesy until great desolation had occurred (Isaiah 6:8–13). God will not continue to let you distract His people, just as He got tired of the sin of the Israelites. Woe to them who do such. Are your methods for disciple making developing persons who actually go forth and make other disciples? Are you a disciple maker producing the fruit of other disciple makers?

Reach Me With SMILES

Ask, Oh Lord, am I distracting Your people, blurring their vision of You? Do the words that I speak draw others to You, or to my issues? Lord, are my actions pleasing to You, or are they barriers that block Your blessings from those who would otherwise become disciples and makers of disciples? Deliver me, Lord, from myself. Discipline me, Lord, that I may learn of You. Develop me into the disciple maker that you have commissioned me to be. Nurture me, Lord, so that I may help others to grow closer to You as I grow closer to You. Nurture me, Lord, while I wait to see You in eternity.

> *I waited patiently for the Lord; And He inclined to me, and heard my cry. He brought me up out of the pit of destruction, out of the miry clay; And He set my feet upon a rock making my footsteps firm. And He put a new song in my mouth, a song of praise to our God; Many will see and fear, And will trust in the Lord. How blessed is the man who has made the Lord his trust, And has not turned to the proud, nor to those who lapse into falsehood.*
>
> —Psalm 40:1–4

Share the Gospel of Jesus Christ!

> *For God so loved the world, that He gave His only begotten Son, that whoever believes in Him should not perish, but have eternal life. For God did not send the Son into the world to judge the world, but that the world should be saved through Him.*
>
> —John 3:16–17

Further Reading

Gray, James M. *First Steps to Understanding Your Bible*. Chicago: Meridian Publication, 1996.

Epilogue

The urgency and seriousness of your conviction to being called to teach and make disciples is an awesome responsibility. Know who you are. Know your purpose. And, know what you are teaching. Read, observe, interpret, and apply Scripture by considering the context of the passage, reading what comes before and after it. Always consider preparation for teaching as a process and develop methods and activities to lift the central theme or single concept to be taught for that lesson. Repeating the learning process is crucial. Furthermore, know the people that you are teaching.

Keep your lessons fresh; stay equipped and current with what God has called you to do. Read and attend training sessions locally, statewide, and nationally, when possible. Stay abreast of methods and materials to remain up to date, and vary the techniques you employ for teaching and learning based on the objective or goal of the passage at hand. Self-evaluate regularly and have confidence. Know that Jesus is able to keep you from falling, as you reach the children of God with SMILES.

How do you teach a Bible lesson that will assist believers with spiritual growth?

Reach Me With SMILES

With S M I L E S!
- Stimulate Me
- Motivate Me
- Involve Me
- Love Me
- Encourage Me
- Strengthen Me

Do this and you will reach me for Christ!

References

Anderson, Lorin W., ed. *International Encyclopedia of Teaching and Teacher Education.* Pergamon, 1995.

Armstrong, Thomas. "Multiple Intelligences in the Classroom," Association for Supervision and Curriculum Development, 2000

Arn, Win and Charles Arn. *The Master's Plan for Making Disciples: Every Christian an Effective Witness through an Enabling Church.* Grand Rapids, Michigan: Baker Books, 1998.

Anderson, Andy. *The Growth Spiral.* Nashville: Broadman and Holman Publishers, 1993.

Johnston, Jay and Ronald Brown. *Teaching the Jesus Way: Building a Transformational Teaching Ministry.* Nashville: LifeWay Press, 2000.

Campbell, Roger. *Staying Positive in a Negative World: Attitudes that*

Enhance the Joy of Living, Grand Rapids, Michigan: Kregel Publications, 1997.

Carlson, Gregory C. *Understanding Teaching: Effective Biblical Teaching*. Wheaton, Illinois: Evangelical Training Association, 1998.

Edge, Findley B. *Teaching for Results*. Nashville: Broadman and Holman Publishers, 1995.

Foster, Charles R. *The Future of Christian Education*. Educating Congregations. Nashville: Abingdon Press, 1994.

Fitch, James E. *Building a Great Church through the Sunday School*, Nashville: Convention Press, 1993.

Garner, Larry and Tony Martin. *Gifts of Grace: Discovering and Using Your Spiritual Gifts*. Jackson Mississippi: Baptist Books, 1995.

Gray, James M. *First Steps to Understanding Your Bible*. Chicago: Meridian Publications, 1996.

Griggs, Donald L. and Judy M. Walther. *Christian Education in the Small Church*, Valley Forge, Pennsylvania: Judson Press, 1992.

Halverson, Delia. *32 Ways to Become A Great Sunday School Teacher*. Nashville: Abingdon Press, 1997.

Hammett, Edward H. *The Gathered and Scattered Church: Equipping Believers for the 21st Century*. Macon, Georgia: Smyth and Helwys, 1999.

Hawkins, Don. *Master Discipleship: Jesus' Prayer and Plan for Every Believer*. Grand Rapids, Michigan: Kregel Resources, 1996.

References

Hawkins, O. S. *Drawing the Net: 30 Practical Principles for Leading Others to Christ* Publicly and Personally. Nashville: Broadman Press, 1993.

Hemphill, Ken. *Revitalizing the Sunday Morning Dinosaur: A Sunday School Growth Strategy for the 21st Century.* Nashville: Broadman and Holman Publishers, 1996.

Henderson, David W. *Culture Shift: Communicating God's Truth to Our Changing World.* Grand Rapids, Michigan: Baker Books, 1999.

Henrichsen, Walter A. *Disciples Are Made Not Born: Equipping Christians to Multiply Themselves through Ministry to Others.* Colorado Springs, Colorado: Chariot Victor Publishing, 1988.

Hunt, Josh. *Disciple-Making Teachers: How to Equip Adults for Growth and Action.* Loveland, Colorado: Group, 1998.

Lingo, Susan L. *Larger-than-Life Activities: Colossal Crafts that Teach and Serve.*Cincinnati: The Standard Publishing Company, 1998.

Malphurs, Aubrey. Strategy 2000: *Churches Making Disciples for the Next Millennium.* Grand Rapids, Michigan: Kregel Publications, 1996.

McCalep, George. *Stir Up the Gifts.* Lithonia, Georgia: Orman Press, 1999.

McQuay, Earl P. *Learning to Study the Bible.* Nashville: Broadman Press, 1992.

Mims, Gene. *Kingdom Principles for Church Growth.* Nashville: Convention Press, 1994.

Nanus, Burt. *Leading the Way to Organization Renewal*. Portland, Oregon: Productivity Press, 1996.

Orlich, Donald C., et. al. *Teaching Strategies: A Guide to Better Instruction*. D. C. Heath, 1980.

Roehlkepartain, Eugene C. *The Teaching Church: Moving Christian Education to Center Stage*, Nashville: Abingdon Press, 1993.

Ryken, Leland, et. al. gen. ed, *Dictionary of Biblical Imagery*. Downers Grove, Illinois: InterVarsity Press, 1998.

Schaller, Lyle E. *21 Bridges to the 21st Century: The Future of Pastoral Ministry*. Nashville: Abingdon Press, 1994.

Shawchuck, Norman and Gustave Rath. *Benchmarks of Quality in the Church: 21 Ways to Continuously Improve the Content of Your Ministry*. Nashville: Abingdon Press, 1994.

Smith, Donald P. *How to Attract and Keep Active Church Members*, Louisville: John Knox Press, 1992.

Stewart, Carlyle F. *African American Church Growth: 12 Principles for Prophetic Ministry*, Nashville: Abingdon Press, 1994.

Taylor, Bill L. *21 Truths, Traditions, and Trends: Propelling the Sunday School into the 21st Century*. Nashville: Convention Press, 1996.

The New National Baptist Hymnal, Nashville: National Baptist Publishing Board, 1974.

Warren, Rick. *The Purpose Driven Church: Growth without Compromising Your Message and Mission*, Grand Rapids, Michigan: Zondervan Publishing House, 1995.

References

Welch, Bobby H. A. *Evangelism through the Sunday School: A Journey of Faith*. Nashville: LifeWay Press, 1997.

Wilhoit, Jim and Ryken. *Effective BIBLE Teaching*. Grand Rapids, Michigan: Baker Book House, 1995.

Willis, Avery Jr. *MasterLife*. Nashville: LifeWay.

Yount, William R. *Called to Teach: An Introduction to the Ministry of Teaching*. Nashville: Broadman and Holman Publishers, 1999.

Wimberly, Anne Streaty. *Soul Stories: African American Christian Education*. Nashville: Abingdon Press, 1994.

Appendix A

Suggested learning activities to enhance reaching believers for lasting spiritual growth.

1. Bible Book Review

State the names of the main characters. Discuss their internal traits (including their ideas, prejudices, emotions, and ambitions).

> What factors are given to show how these personality traits were molded?
>
> What is the setting?
>
> What is the prevailing, or general mood of the book—humorous, sad, despairing, hopeful, etc.? Explain why.
>
> What is the writer's stated purpose for writing this book?
>
> What is your personal reaction to the book?
>
> What basic problem do the people face?
>
> How do they manage to solve that problem or respond to that problem?

Reach Me With SMILES

What main thought does the writer attempt to impress upon the reader?

What personal opinions or interests of the writer do you detect in the book?

What lessons do you learn from the book?

Summarize the book in you own words.

2. Sensory Images from Sensory Details

Use the senses to feel the words of the passage being read for deeper spiritual meaning.

Smell
Sight
Taste
Hearing
Touch (feeling)
Emotion (feeling)

3. Reading the Bible from Another Angle

Use any of these ideas to enhance lesson development on specific passages. (The suggestions that follow are not intended to be combined for one lesson.)

Writing focus:

- How is the passage organized?
- How does the writer develop ideas?
- What specific words reveal the context?
- Identify multiple meanings through situations, sensory images, similes, metaphors, dialogue.
- Identify the various types of writing employed (prose, poetry, metaphoric, etc.)
- Identify the types of sentences used, e.g., statement, question, command, etc.
- How are various sentences structured? What kinds of words that are used for particular functions:

Appendix A

Subject	-	Who is doing something
Predicate	-	What the subject is doing
Noun	-	Name, person, place, thing, idea
Verb	-	Action, state that something is in existence (state of being)
Adjective/adverb	-	Describes

(Do not get too technical here. Restrict the use of this strategy to what naturally flows from the passage. Do not force it.)

4. What can I do to be a better church member?
   Read Hebrews 10:19–25 then write your response.

_____
_____
_____
_____
_____
_____
_____
_____

Appendix B

A. How do you teach a Bible lesson that will assist believers with spiritual growth?

Know what you are teaching and why you are teaching it.

Enrich the lesson.

Emphasize results—specific aims, goals, and objectives

Be intentional about knowing the groundwork of each lesson for yourself.

Establish a baseline with personal study.

Be self-directed.

Be continual and consistent.

Be informed (in-home library, refresher readings, workshops).

Evaluate yourself: "I recognize that I am part of the learning process, not the center."

Pray in the classroom (Do you use prayer only to open and close each session?).

Invite others to observe and critique you. Observe others.

Reach Me With SMILES

Plan for preparation.

Evaluate your time management. (Is it effective?)

Evaluate your lesson planning. (Which part of your lesson is strongest/weakest?)

Use questions to stimulate discussion. (Do you write them down as part of your lesson plan?)

Review for age appropriateness. (Are the activities right for the group?)

Consider positive and negative communication (verbal and nonverbal).

B. How do you teach a Bible lesson that will assist believers with spiritual growth? Remember these things:

A variety of approaches draws the most out of believers.

Varied teaching techniques give students multiple opportunities to use the lesson to help someone else.

Practical application makes the greatest impact.

Discussion, games, and role playing draw students deeper into the lesson.

Visual displays or learning centers bring lessons to life.

Appropriate use of technology can illuminate a lesson.

Simultaneous discussion teams (2–3 persons) allow for greater participation.

Visual or audio aids, such as pictures, objects, or music, can represent concepts.

Resource files from Lenten seasons, Advent, and other events can generate ideas.

Teachable moments present themselves through everyday events, crises, celebrations, current events, news stories, etc.

Appendix B

Questioning is more effective than lecturing.

Performance activities get students involved beyond the classroom.

Projects put classroom lessons into action for all ages.

Personal application is portable.

Cooperative learning builds relationships.

Intergenerational learning breeds understanding.

Service oriented projects bring the Gospel to life.

Appendix C

Survey Questions

During several seminars and workshops held between 1999 and 2001, I surveyed participants to find out their thoughts on a few ideas relating to Christian education. These results represent responses from urban and rural, smaller and larger churches throughout the state of Virginia. After compiling the comments from various surveys, it became clear to me that people have different ideas about the functions that religious organizations serve and roles various leaders play. Knowing the diversity of opinions held within the same organization has helped me to transform my approach as I continue to serve God. I offer some suggestions that will assist in planning more effective ministries as a result of reviewing the responses. See if you can offer more ideas.

Ideas for More Effective Teaching
- Give a variety of classes; offer a variety of styles of lesson presentation to encourage more adults, youth and children to participate. People are hungry for depth and want more time for class.

- Consider having fellowship opportunities where lessons can be continued over lunch one Saturday per quarter, or coffee one evening, in addition to the regular time, for example.
- Take the time necessary to study and plan well. Some lessons are boring because the teachers are last-minute preparers. It is difficult to motivate someone to do something that you are not willing to do yourself. Dynamic lessons take time to plan. Workers' meetings can highlight techniques for teaching lessons. The meetings can also dig deeper into the scriptural text using PERCS (See page 18),
- Other

_____
_____
_____
_____
_____

Survey Responses

The bulleted lists that follow are verbatim survey responses.

- *What keeps you involved in the church?*

    Love

    Love for Christ

    Commitment to duty

    Need to hear the Word

    Fellowship with others; Connect with other believers

    Desire for spiritual growth through

    Spiritual empowerment

    What can be done to prevent you from wanting to quit [involvement in a church]?

    Never wanted to quit

    Prayer and faith

Appendix C

A deeper and abiding faith

Effective prayer for greater tolerance

Keeping prayed up and in the Word

Communication: talking to someone who has past experience

- *Describe the duties of a Sunday School Superintendent*

    Organizing activities, presiding over Sunday School or a weekly Bible Study, or weekly Bible Study Workers' meetings, communicating with pastor and joint boards

    Coordinator of Sunday School or weekly Bible Study classes, programs, 59–80 members in Sunday School or a weekly Bible Study or a weekly Bible Study

    Select teachers, teacher lesson plans

    Be on time – be in charge of the Sunday School or a weekly Bible Study or a weekly Bible Study as a whole

    Leading the people, otherwise the supervision (in charge of meetings)

    Open Sunday School or a weekly Bible Study on time and remark short so lesson can be tougher

    Act as the head person for correlating the teaching activities of the Sunday School or a weekly Bible Study or weekly Bible Study teachers

    New – need guidance on the duties

    Open the school, make sure the teachers are there

    Try to teach and help teachers, to educate them on the Word of God and to develop Christian growth

    Plan, organize, keep teachers informed, motivated, humble, open to God's instructions

    Coordinates the work of the Sunday School or a weekly

Reach Me With SMILES

Bible Study or a weekly Bible Study

To be overall in charge (under the pastor) of the Sunday School or a weekly Bible Study or a weekly Bible Study Program and select and train teachers

Oversee smooth operation of the Sunday School or a weekly Bible Study or a weekly Bible Study, assist teachers when needed, promote the Sunday School or a weekly Bible Study

- *Describe the duties of a Sunday School Union President*
  Preside over BTU meetings

  Meet with other union presidents and plan with them what they anticipate on doing for the year and agree with one another

  The main person that gives information as to what should be done by the superintendents

  To plan, coordinate and conduct an annual BTU and Sunday School or a weekly Bible Study or a Bible Study convention

  Not sure about the union: it hosts two day sessions during months with five Sundays with business and training workshops on Saturday and worship with host church on Sunday, available for training workshops throughout the year

- *Describe the duties of an association leader*
  Plan meetings, programs, etc. Visit other churches and associations to see what they are doing. Prepare for the association that meet each year for 1 or 2 days at different churches to listen to sermons, seminars, youth programs, etc. (the annual convention)

[NOTE: Many areas do not have active regional bodies for training.]

Appendix C

- *List your top five (5) training needs.* [Training occurred in the majority of the responses.]

    The workshops that have a skilled, knowledgeable spirit-filled trainer that knows what they are really there for and teaching

    Even trained and spirit-led teachers need to be refreshed from time to time

    Willing persons that will come forth to be trained

    Group training - getting teachers together making sure they are teaching the same thing

    Equipping the superintendent to serve effectively, as well as the other church school officers

    Training teachers to be teacher and getting them to attend lesson review sessions

    Teacher workshops - focusing on responsibilities as teachers of the Word

    Sunday School or a weekly Bible Study or a weekly Bible Study training class and discussion of lesson each week

    Training for superintendents so they can help the teachers/associates to be more effective teachers or leaders

    Training or knowing what source of materials should be purchased

    Training on effective Vacation Bible School, presentation

    Train teachers to teach

    Training the superintendent/leaders

    Training in age-appropriate activities and how to discover your gifts in this particular area

    Train teachers to use the Bible and reference materials

    Superintendents need workshop training together

Training needed to let Sunday School or weekly Bible Study members know that all Teachers should be addressing the same lesson training others

Scripture teaching and teachers training in presentation of the information

The importance of Scripture was the second most prevalent response

stress importance of studying Scripture

Learning the Word of God

How to apply the Word to our lives and the people we work with

Overall let everyone know we must be trained and study God's Word in order to please God

Study Scripture at all time each and every day

Need improved methods of presenting the Scripture to the different age groups

All other responses are listed with no particular hierarchy.

Understanding lesson so it can be explained to the class

Give class assignments to bring to the group on the following Sunday

We need to learn to stay in our area or function in your gift where we can remain effective and stop being legends in our own minds

Ability to accept change

Adequate space and materials

I need ways to motivate teachers to attend Bible study and seminars

How to use time more wisely

Getting needed support from the pastoral staff

Appendix C

To have more of a knowledge base on how to find "good" information

How to get more class participation

Productive responses

Need to know how to motivate people in the doing of God's Word.

Better book for 8–15 age

Ways to motivate people

Ways to get believers interested and study the Word

Age-appropriate classes

Chalk boards (portable), hands on material, more training aids (bulletin boards, overhead projectors, videos)

Planning classes for all youth teachers – 3–10 age group

Listening to what is asked and understanding it before you answer

How to apply the lesson to today

How to avoid arguing a point

Being receptive to others understanding or interpretation of the lesson

Setting up the classroom for maximum effect/techniques

How to improve my leadership skills

Basic teaching skills – time management

Bible interpretation and Baptist beliefs

Discipline - maintaining order

Teachers need to exercise their ability to keep the class (youth 16–23) focused on the Sunday School or a weekly Bible Study lesson, getting rooted in the Word, making everyone feel like they are important (lesson review sessions)

Reach Me With SMILES

Teachers that are willing to teach, will study to teach and be on time

More space in which to conduct classes, (closed rooms to reduce distraction)

Church leaders to attend Sunday School or a weekly Bible Study or a weekly Bible Study (to set the example)

Superintendents

Program leaders

Teach the children and also some adults how to stand when speaking

Would like a method to make Sunday School or a weekly Bible Study more exciting

Need the leaders of our church in Bible teaching and study so as to be more in the Word of God

"I'm not going to that class" - not willing to "sit under his teaching"

A teacher's assistant program

All do same teaching

Be able to talk to each other with the same voice from one day to another

New or tried methods to involve quiet/don't like to talk individuals

Leaders' Reflections Survey Results
- *How does the role of your group's leader effect and affect the growth of the Sunday School and the overall teaching ministry of the church?*

   Set the tone

   Positive manner

   A great deal - when we lost our pastor due to death, the

Appendix C

Sunday School or a weekly Bible Study kept the faith

Improve Bible knowledge and understanding

Good

I'm hopefully only a wheel in the middle of a hub

Make everyone aware that we can grow by faith

There is little to no growth

It's a priority

- *What does your group do that really works to enhance the growth of the Sunday School or a weekly Bible Study?*

  Makes everyone feel a part of the group

  Promote participation

  Evangelize, recognized those who have brought the most to Christ with dinner tickets

  Allows believers to expand on the Word through individual expression

  Learn how to take to the teacher

  Plan programs - activities

  Show how to act towards one another

  Sunday School or a weekly Bible Study Promotion Day held as well as promotion by Superintendent on 4th Sundays

  How is that growth measured?

  Participation and action

  Believers become teachers

  Quarterly evaluation

  Participation

  By people participation

Reach Me With SMILES

By attendance

By the attendance and the enthusiasm of the Sunday School or a weekly Bible Study or a weekly Bible Study

Spirituality

- *How does your group motivate the participation of others?*

    Zeal bring on more zeal in others

    Making them feel

    Assign different responsibilities

    Allow each student to express him/herself

    By active participation

    Little is done to motivate our Sunday School or a weekly Bible Study

    Encouraging to use talents

- *What can your group do differently to stimulate greater participation of others?*

    More outreach

    Need to plan

    Let them know they are much needed

    Love and accept one another as Christ loved us

    The bringing together of the occupations

    Letting people have a chance to do something different

    be more active

    Change some of the officers

- *What is God doing in your group or through your group?*

    Increasing knowledge and understanding

    Taking us to new levels as growth allows

Appendix C

Letting us know He is in charge

Allowing the church to grow in His grace

Helping teachers to grow spiritually through learning to search the Scriptures

Teaching obedience

Showing us how to get along

- *What is wrong with your Sunday School or weekly Bible Study?*
  Not everyone has been reached

  Needs to be promoted

  Getting all to be on time and supporting in giving their monies

  Not long enough to finish each lesson

  Lack of teacher effectiveness

  Not starting on time

  Not enough adult participation

  I am not certain.

  Low attendance

- *What is right with your Sunday School or weekly Bible Study?*
  Teaching the Word with excitement

  Willing leaders

  Several good teachers

  Lifts up our Lord and Savior Jesus Christ

  Committed Christian members who continue to pray and support the Sunday School or a weekly Bible Study

  The faithful few

  The length of time allocated (9:30–11:00)

Reach Me With SMILES

   That we are blessed to have the ones we have

   Sunday School or weekly Bible Study workers meetings monthly, pastor support

- *What are the challenges and issues you face with the Sunday School or a weekly Bible Study?*

   Keeping the people stimulated

   Pastor not attending

   AIDS, teen mothers

   Keeping everyone on one accord

   Need for teachers and teacher training

- *What will your Sunday School or a weekly Bible Study look like in the next millennium?*

   Even better with the help of the Lord

   Looking to the Lord

   Trusting God will help us where we need the help

   It is declining now; hopefully it will grow through the training in the Word.

   I hope a 100% attendance rate.

   Crowded with love

   Good servants minister what they have with servant love.

Appendix C

Points to Ponder

What is happening in our churches if the leaders have difficulty articulating what it is that God is doing through them? What does the Bible say happens to a tree that does not bear good fruit? It seems that we are not sure what we are growing.

Bear fruit worthy of repentance. Do not presume to say to yourselves, 'We have Abraham as our ancestor'; for I tell you, God is able from theses stones to raise up children to Abraham. Even now the ax is lying at the root of the trees; every tree therefore that does not bear good fruit is cut down and thrown into the fire. —Matthew 4:8–10

God can raise up a stone. Don't let His axe cut down your tree!

Survey Conclusion

Leaders need regular training sessions that will enable them to train others for evangelism, fulfilling the Great Commission.

Christian educators need to be very intentional about demonstrating effective teaching techniques and resources that will reach the people where they are. They know what they need and we should feel an obligation to go and teach all of them wherever they are.

There is a tremendous need for creative teaching techniques that will reach God's people in the future. Techniques are still being used that were innovative at the turn of the 20th century, but are no longer.

Many people are crying out for help in revitalizing Christian education ministries. Approximately half of those who responded to the survey teach in their local church.

Many leaders appear to be program oriented rather than ministry focused. Our leaders are very busy; but what are they busy doing? Are they simply running an organization or truly meeting the needs of an organism?

The leaders did not identify many things that they do that are measurable; the statements are vague.

The leaders are not in consensus regarding the duties and responsibilities of Sunday School superintendents, Sunday School union presidents, and association leaders.

Leaders are gathering people together, but not equipping them to be scattered for ministry beyond the doors of the church.

Booking Information and Orders

Barbara Brehon is available for teaching and preaching engagements for your church or organization. For scheduling information, call:

(757) 848-1088 or (757) 647-5418
or email
Vbscstatedirecto@aol.com

To order copies of *Reach Me With SMILES* for yourself, your church, or organization, please complete the form below.

Reach Me With SMILES ORDER FORM

Name _____

Phone _____ Email _____

Church/Org. _____

Shipping Address _____

City, State, Zip _____

Number of copies   _____
*($19.95 +$4.05 shipping & handling)**   @ $24.00 each

Total enclosed $ _____

* Special pricing is available for group orders or events.

> Make check or money order to:
>
> Dr. Barbara A. F. Brehon
> 6 Mizzen Circle
> Hampton, VA 23664

Thank you for your order. Please allow 4–6 weeks for delivery.